Extending Ansible

Discover how to efficiently deploy and customize
Ansible in the way your platform demands

Rishabh Das

BIRMINGHAM - MUMBAI

Extending Ansible

First published: March 2016

Production reference: 1210316

Published by Packt Publishing Ltd.
Livery Place
35 Livery Street
Birmingham B3 2PB, UK.

ISBN 978-1-78217-500-1

www.packtpub.com

Credits

Author
Rishabh Das

Reviewer
Xiang Zhang

Commissioning Editor
Veena Pagare

Acquisition Editor
Subho Gupta

Content Development Editor
Divij Kotian

Technical Editor
Vivek Pala

Copy Editor
Lauren Harkins

Project Coordinator
Nikhil Nair

Proofreader
Safis Editing

Indexer
Tejal Soni

Graphics
Kirk D'Penha

Production Coordinator
Melwyn D'sa

Cover Work
Melwyn D'sa

About the Author

Rishabh Das, presently working with Red Hat India, is responsible for managing and maintaining the CI/CD workflow and infrastructure for his team. He has more than 3 years of industry experience and has extensive hands-on experience with Ansible. You can reach Rishabh on Twitter at @rshbhdas.

This book would have not seen the light of day without the support of many individuals—both known and unknown. I would like to express my gratitude to the Ansible and Python communities for making my life easier. Thank you to everyone who is part of this open source community for all the amazing work that you do.

I would like to thank my colleagues who helped me out at each step with their varying abilities. I couldn't have asked for more encouragement and support. Thank you for all the awesome projects you work on, giving me an opportunity to learn, explore, and push my limits.

Thanks to my friends and family, who have always been there no matter the time, situation, or place. Thanks for all the things you have done, for all the ideas you pitched in, for my craziness that you put up with, and for all the compromises you made to help me finish off what I started.

Lastly, but most importantly, I want to specially thank my father, who every single day, checked on my progress. I couldn't have reached this far without you. Thank you ma and baba.

About the Reviewer

Xiang Zhang is a systems engineer working for SINA. He has expertise in Python and has put Ansible in use to manage several thousand servers at work.

SINA is a NASDAQ-listed company and the parent company of Weibo, another NASDAQ-listed company.

www.PacktPub.com

eBooks, discount offers, and more

Did you know that Packt offers eBook versions of every book published, with PDF and ePub files available? You can upgrade to the eBook version at `www.PacktPub.com` and as a print book customer, you are entitled to a discount on the eBook copy. Get in touch with us at `customercare@packtpub.com` for more details.

At `www.PacktPub.com`, you can also read a collection of free technical articles, sign up for a range of free newsletters and receive exclusive discounts and offers on Packt books and eBooks.

`https://www2.packtpub.com/books/subscription/packtlib`

Do you need instant solutions to your IT questions? PacktLib is Packt's online digital book library. Here, you can search, access, and read Packt's entire library of books.

Why subscribe?

- Fully searchable across every book published by Packt
- Copy and paste, print, and bookmark content
- On demand and accessible via a web browser

Table of Contents

Preface

With most companies moving to the cloud, infrastructure needs are growing exponentially. The growing data and massive computing power required to store, analyze, and process this data adds to the infrastructure needs. With the endlessly increasing number of Internet service users and the enormous inflow of data accompanied by a race for data mining, big data and cloud services have opened up new data centers and expanded upon the existing ones. Also, with constantly scaling infrastructure and increasing demands, with the 99.9% uptime promises to keep, automated management of infrastructure became the need of the hour. DevOps soon became a necessity and the market has flooded with DevOps tools. Ansible is one such open source solution that combines orchestration, configuration management, and application deployment capabilities in one.

Ansible is an IT automation tool that lets you manage your Infrastructure as Code. It helps you deploy your applications and manage configurations, thus making life easier. It is an open source project built on Python and has great community support. Ansible, in most ways, is sufficient to address most of your requirements. With a number of modules and plugins available, Ansible makes everything look so easy. Writing and understanding playbooks is smooth.

This book is aimed at advanced users who already have a working knowledge of Ansible, we will discuss various extension points that are exposed by Ansible and how they can be exploited to fit our requirements. This book covers in detail the Ansible Python API, Ansible modules, and Ansible plugins. In this book—by means of real-life scenarios—demonstrates how Ansible can be extended to meet your requirements. This will take you through a step-by-step process of how you can fill in the gaps and become a master of Ansible.

What this book covers

Chapter 1, *Getting Started with Ansible*, is an introductory chapter that introduces you to Ansible and encourages you to become a power user. It introduces you to the Ansible architecture and gives you a reason to chose Ansible as an infrastructure and configuration management tool.

Chapter 2, *Getting to Know Ansible Modules*, covers the basics of writing an Ansible module. It introduces you to the AnsibleModule boilerplate. This chapter also helps you develop sample Ansible modules in Bash and Python.

Chapter 3, *Digging Deeper into Ansible Modules*, introduces you to handling arguments in an Ansible Module. It also takes you through a scenario of collecting information about the infrastructure by developing a custom Ansible module.

Chapter 4, *Exploring API*, covers in detail the Python API for Ansible, running Ansible programmatically, and discusses the various extension points provided by Ansible. It discusses topics such as Plugin Loader, Runner, Playbooks, and Callbacks in depth.

Chapter 5, *An In-Depth Look at Ansible Plugins*, covers different plugins from the code level. It also demonstrates how you can write your own Ansible plugin through a few examples.

Chapter 6, *Fitting It All Together – Integration*, covers various configuration options for Ansible, thus allowing the user to get the most out of the tool. This chapter introduces you to Ansible Galaxy, a platform for sharing roles. It takes the reader through the process of contributing to Ansible and distributing their modules and plugins.

Chapter 7, *Becoming a Master – A Complete Configuration Guide*, contains real-life scenarios where one can exploit the power of Ansible to perform the required tasks. Also contains scenarios where one can go a step ahead from using Ansible as an Infrastructure and configuration management tool.

What you need for this book

To get the most out of this book, you need the following:

- Linux distribution (Fedora/Ubuntu)
- Ansible
- Python

Who this book is for

This book is perfect for developers and administrators who are familiar with Ansible and Python programming but have no knowledge of how to customize Ansible.

Conventions

In this book, you will find a number of text styles that distinguish between different kinds of information. Here are some examples of these styles and an explanation of their meaning.

Code words in text, database table names, folder names, filenames, file extensions, pathnames, dummy URLs, user input, and Twitter handles are shown as follows: "A path specified by the `library` variable in the configuration file, located at `/etc/ansible/ansible.cfg`."

A block of code is set as follows:

```
[default]
exten => s,1,Dial(Zap/1|30)
exten => s,2,Voicemail(u100)
exten => s,102,Voicemail(b100)
exten => i,1,Voicemail(s0)
```

When we wish to draw your attention to a particular part of a code block, the relevant lines or items are set in bold:

```
[default]
exten => s,1,Dial(Zap/1|30)
exten => s,2,Voicemail(u100)
exten => s,102,Voicemail(b100)
exten => i,1,Voicemail(s0)
```

Any command-line input or output is written as follows:

```
# cp /usr/src/asterisk-addons/configs/cdr_mysql.conf.sample
    /etc/asterisk/cdr_mysql.conf
```

New terms and **important words** are shown in bold. Words that you see on the screen, for example, in menus or dialog boxes, appear in the text like this: "By using the **Add a Role** option from the menu and supplying the required credentials, Galaxy will import the role from your GitHub repository and make it available on the Galaxy platform for the entire community."

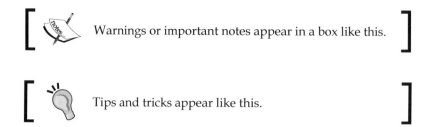

Warnings or important notes appear in a box like this.

Tips and tricks appear like this.

Reader feedback

Feedback from our readers is always welcome. Let us know what you think about this book—what you liked or disliked. Reader feedback is important for us as it helps us develop titles that you will really get the most out of.

To send us general feedback, simply e-mail feedback@packtpub.com, and mention the book's title in the subject of your message.

If there is a topic that you have expertise in and you are interested in either writing or contributing to a book, see our author guide at www.packtpub.com/authors.

Customer support

Now that you are the proud owner of a Packt book, we have a number of things to help you to get the most from your purchase.

Downloading the example code

You can download the example code files for this book from your account at http://www.packtpub.com. If you purchased this book elsewhere, you can visit http://www.packtpub.com/support and register to have the files e-mailed directly to you.

You can download the code files by following these steps:

1. Log in or register to our website using your e-mail address and password.
2. Hover the mouse pointer on the **SUPPORT** tab at the top.
3. Click on **Code Downloads & Errata**.
4. Enter the name of the book in the **Search** box.
5. Select the book for which you're looking to download the code files.
6. Choose from the drop-down menu where you purchased this book from.
7. Click on **Code Download**.

Once the file is downloaded, please make sure that you unzip or extract the folder using the latest version of:

- WinRAR / 7-Zip for Windows
- Zipeg / iZip / UnRarX for Mac
- 7-Zip / PeaZip for Linux

Errata

Although we have taken every care to ensure the accuracy of our content, mistakes do happen. If you find a mistake in one of our books—maybe a mistake in the text or the code—we would be grateful if you could report this to us. By doing so, you can save other readers from frustration and help us improve subsequent versions of this book. If you find any errata, please report them by visiting `http://www.packtpub. com/submit-errata`, selecting your book, clicking on the **Errata Submission Form** link, and entering the details of your errata. Once your errata are verified, your submission will be accepted and the errata will be uploaded to our website or added to any list of existing errata under the Errata section of that title.

To view the previously submitted errata, go to `https://www.packtpub.com/books/ content/support` and enter the name of the book in the search field. The required information will appear under the **Errata** section.

Piracy

Piracy of copyrighted material on the Internet is an ongoing problem across all media. At Packt, we take the protection of our copyright and licenses very seriously. If you come across any illegal copies of our works in any form on the Internet, please provide us with the location address or website name immediately so that we can pursue a remedy.

Please contact us at `copyright@packtpub.com` with a link to the suspected pirated material.

We appreciate your help in protecting our authors and our ability to bring you valuable content.

Questions

If you have a problem with any aspect of this book, you can contact us at `questions@packtpub.com`, and we will do our best to address the problem.

1
Getting Started with Ansible

As technology has advanced, computing has become more and more complex. With better hardware being manufactured each day, the complexity of computing systems has increased. Distributed computing started flourishing, and soon "the cloud" was invented. Software became trivial and managing it became a pain. Development cycles picked up the pace, and manual testing and deployments soon felt outdated, hence calling for automation. If you are reading this book, you probably understand the importance of automation, be it for testing an application or managing the whole infrastructure.

With increasing load and ever-scaling infrastructure, system administrators have stopped being simple craftspeople by configuring each system manually and have begun to manage thousands of systems at once. For any environment, however big it is, you need a reliable system to manage it all. The geographically scattered workplaces and ever-growing infrastructure make it nearly impossible to keep track of the inventory and manually configure and manage each machine. The paced development cycles and reduced time to market leaves little margin for error and throws the manual process out the window.

The key to managing the whole infrastructure, deploying builds, speeding up the process, and at the same time keeping track of the changes is to have a system that is user-friendly, has a small learning curve, and is pluggable as per your requirements. What's most important is that you stay focused and spend more time managing your infrastructure and the processes rather than the automation scripts and management tool itself. Out of the many available solutions, Ansible is one such tool with many interesting features. It is easy to extend and works out of the box for 90% of user requirements. This book focuses on the remaining 10%.

In this chapter, we will be exploring:

- Why Ansible?
- Why extend Ansible?
- The Ansible architecture
- Extending Ansible

Why Ansible?

Out of the many available tools in the market, how do you choose which tool best fits your need? What factors should you consider while choosing a tool to satisfy your requirements? Questions may come to mind such as:

- What is the **return on investment (ROI)** in terms of money, time, and effort?
- What kind of support do I get with the tool?
- What are the potential associated security risks?
- Is the tool flexible enough to be plugged into my infrastructure?
- What is the coverage? Are all my requirements addressed?

If these are the questions that come to mind, I'll try answering them in favor of Ansible.

- Ansible is free. The only investment you need is some time and effort. Ansible playbooks are YAML-based and hence are very easy to read, understand, and maintain, thus involving a very small learning curve. Modules hide the complexity underneath.

- Ansible is open source. Hence, there is an entire community to back you up. You can file in issues or even fix them yourself, since you will always have access to the code.

- Unlike other solutions, which are mostly agent-based, Ansible works purely on SSH. There is no agent required. Therefore, you can sit back and relax, as there is no extra package lying on your production system.

- Ansible provides a very good API, which you can use to build your own Ansible modules that suit your needs and can then be plugged into your infrastructure.

- Ansible provides 90% of user requirements out of the box. The remaining 10% has a well-documented API and community support to build your own modules, hence increasing the coverage.

If you are satisfied by the above arguments and willing to give Ansible a try, read on.

Why extend Ansible?

Ansible comes in handy in various contexts – as a configuration management tool and deployment automation tool, as well as for provisioning and orchestration. It comes out of the box with a lot of plugins and modules that can be used for building playbooks. You can manage your entire infrastructure using Ansible in the way most software development projects do. **Infrastructure as Code (IAC)** applies the same principles of software development to configuration management.

People like Ansible for its simplicity and clear separation of concerns. It doesn't force you to adhere to one particular vision of how you should manage your configurations. It provides a perfect building block for designing your IAC solution, tailored to your specific requirements.

There can be many reasons to extend Ansible. This might range from adding missing features to modifying/enhancing existing features as per your own needs. With Ansible being an open source, community driven project, not everything can be integrated at once. There is always a trade-off between utility and demand. If there are not many users of one particular feature, it becomes an overhead for the project maintainer to support it.

Need something new

So, you come across a situation where Ansible, in its native form with the available modules and plugins, is not enough to meet your requirements. What do you do? Change the tool? Look for other options? Maybe even curse your bad luck for not being able to foresee what was coming and now you need to change everything?

Well, the answer is NO. Ansible provides a very good API and boilerplate that you can use to write your own Ansible modules or plugins as per your requirements. Building Ansible modules is easy. Since Ansible is community driven, you might even file a feature request for the required module if you feel more people are likely to face the same issue you encountered. If you are a developer, you can simply write your own Ansible module or plugin and share it with the community. Send in a pull request for your module and get into a discussion with the project maintainers. Hopefully, the module will be merged and made available in future releases of Ansible.

In this book, we will see how to extend Ansible as per the requirements and distribute the customizations by contributing to an open source project, specifically, Ansible.

Company-wide abstraction

Treating your infrastructure as code offers many advantages, but it comes with a cost. Not all members of your team will be willing to climb the learning curve. As a result, only a few people will become powerful users of any configuration management tool such as Ansible, and they will become the bottleneck for the whole team.

A good IAC implementation should make it easy for everyone to interact with the infrastructure, deploy new software, provision resources, and weave components together. Details should be abstracted away as much as possible, behavior should be clear, and definitions should be navigable. There should also exist an easy way to trace any problems back to a high-level configuration.

To achieve this, one can develop plugins and modules that can abstract the details and provide interfaces that people can directly use and get results from. This will help everyone get up to speed and interact with the infrastructure.

You can create modules and plugins that can make your routine tasks easy. You can share these as utilities that can be used by anyone in the company to carry out similar tasks. This would require some developer efforts, but would enable even the not so powerful users to get the most out of their infrastructure.

Diving into Ansible

Infrastructure grows gradually to a point where you finally give up managing it manually and begin to feel the need for a better way to manage the emergent complexity.

One way to do this is to spend a lot of time looking for the right tool, then you end up adopting a complete configuration management solution, and bend over backwards to change your problem in order to make it fit into the existing solution. Obviously, this approach sounds flawed.

Another approach is to keep it simple and incrementally exploit the power of existing tools when they actually give you an immediate advantage.

Ansible is more suited for the latter approach. It is well-written and offers a clear separation of concerns and a simple model. In fact, you can choose to what degree you want to engage with it. It allows you to reuse components provided by the community while remaining in control.

You can exploit the various extension points exposed by Ansible to build modules and plugins that suit your needs. Reusing already existing plugins and modules and creating your own as and when required provides even more control over your infrastructure.

Contributing to Ansible

Ansible is an open source project hosted on GitHub. If you have a GitHub account, you can easily fork the Ansible repository and start contributing to the project (Ansible code: `https://github.com/ansible/ansible`).

You can fork the project in your own account, clone it, and then make changes and send out pull requests to the project owner. This applies to all the open source projects.

If you don't know where to start contributing, you can also look at the *Issues* section in the repository. The *Issues* section contains bug reports and feature requests from people using the tool. You might choose to verify and fix the issues and then send in your patch to the project owner as a pull request against an issue.

The patches go through a review process, and only after the project maintainer's approval, the patch will be merged. Once merged, the feature will then be available to the users.

Ansible architecture

Even though we assume our readers have a working knowledge of Ansible, it is useful to run through a brief overview of the Ansible architecture, so as to have a better understanding of the various extension points.

Ansible is an agentless configuration management system, meaning no special software has to run on the managed hosts. Ansible connects to its targets usually via plain SSH, copies all the necessary code, and runs it on the target machine. Being agentless is one of the main advantages of Ansible over other solutions. This reduces the overhead of the setup of agents required on the target machines, also reducing security risks, as no extra packages or agents need to be installed.

The core Ansible components include:

- **Inventory**: Target
- **Variables**: Information about the target hosts
- **Connection**: How to talk to the target hosts
- **Runner**: Connect to the target and execute actions
- **Playbook**: Recipe to be executed on the target host
- **Facts**: Dynamic information about the target
- **Modules**: Code that implements actions
- **Callback**: Collects the results of the playbook actions

The following figure shows the architecture of Ansible:

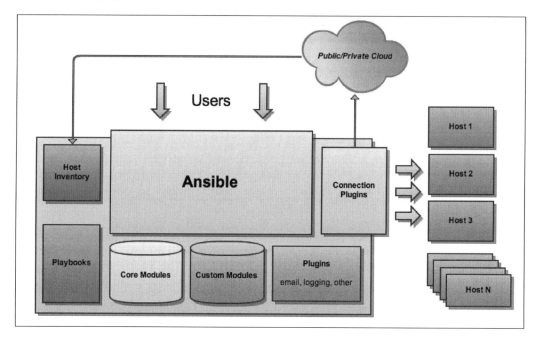

Brief overview of Ansible components

Let's have a closer look at the Ansible components.

Ansible runner

At the heart of Ansible is the **runner**. The runner allows you to execute actions on one or more hosts and gather results.

The runner uses an inventory to choose which hosts to connect to. An inventory may also associate a set of variables with each host. These variables can then be accessed through the playbook and by other Ansible components like the connection plugin.

Connection plugins

Connection plugins (with a default SSH connection) can use specific host variables to figure out how to connect to the remote host. Variables may include information like a username to be used to connect to the remote host, a non-default port number, and so on.

Playbook

Moving on to another component, the **playbook** is one of the most important, as all the recipes are written in the form of Ansible playbooks. Playbooks are modeled as a collection of plays, each of which defines a set of tasks to be executed on a group of remote hosts. A play also defines the environment where the tasks will be executed.

Roles

Playbook can be broken down into **roles** for better organization. Roles help in modularizing the playbook tasks. These roles can later be included in the play against specific host groups. For instance, if your infrastructure involves web servers and proxy servers, each requiring a common set of tasks (preparing the systems) and then type-specific tasks (setting up and configuring web/proxy servers), these can be simply broken down into roles, which can later be run against specific hosts. Common tasks can be defined against all hosts, at which time webserver and proxy server roles can then be executed against respective host groups.

Variables

Another important component in Ansible architecture is **variables**. Variables can be used to extract common values and parameterize shared playbook fragments. They can also be used to categorize hosts based on some quality they share.

Facts

Since every host can give out a lot of information about itself, managing them manually is not a recommended practice. Hence, Ansible included a special variable called **facts** in its software.

The facts variable is provided by the setup module and gets implicitly executed on every host (unless explicitly disabled). This variable collects information about the remote host before the runner starts the execution of the playbook on the remote hosts.

Runner

Now that we have the Ansible playbook in place and all facts about the remote host group have been collected, the runner kicks in. The runner variable executes the specific actions (as specified in the Ansible playbook) on the remote hosts by copying the action code to the target machine and preparing the environment before executing the action code.

Once the runner evaluates and executes the tasks, it cleans up the copied code from the remote host, finally reporting the status through **callbacks**.

Playbook expressiveness

The expressiveness of the playbook language is limited in order to promote a somewhat declarative and descriptive structure of your configuration. However, Ansible does not go overboard in trying to model a strictly declarative configuration. Ansible plays are modeled as a sequential execution of tasks, affected only by variables.

There are several tricks that allow you to insert complex logic within the playbooks, as well as some extension points, which we will see later, that allow you to achieve what you desire.

Extending Ansible

Ansible provides various extension points that can be used to extend Ansible and fit it to customize your needs. It has four main entry points where you can put in your code:

- **Custom fact scripts**: gathers custom facts from remote hosts
- **Ansible modules**: actuators of actual infrastructure changes
- **Plugins**: extends the Ansible execution life cycle
- **Python API**: inverts the control and exploits parts of Ansible from your custom tools

Custom fact scripts

Dynamic inventories may provide some knowledge about the infrastructure and how it's grouped and managed, but it does not provide a view of the actual state of things.

Before every Ansible run, facts are gathered about the infrastructure against which the playbook is executed. This collects a lot of information about the hosts and can be later used in the Ansible playbook itself, if required.

However, you may find yourself in a position where the default facts gathered as part of the fact-gathering process are not enough. To tackle this, Ansible allows you to run your custom code as part of the fact-gathering phase, right before the Ansible play execution.

Modules

Modules define the primitive operations that can be performed on your infrastructure. They allow you to exactly describe what to do right from the playbook. They can encapsulate a complex high-level task, such as interacting with some external infrastructure component, and deploy a virtual machine or whole environment.

Modules are the key to Ansible customization. Modules can be written in any programming language, and if suitable, they can use Ansible itself to perform the nitty-gritty details of their operation.

A substantial part of this book is devoted to building Ansible modules.

Plugins

The term **plugin** groups a number of extension points that hook deeply in the Ansible core and extend its behavior in powerful ways.

The currently available plugins for Ansible are as follows:

- Action plugins
- Loopback plugins
- Callback plugins
- Connection plugins
- Filter plugins
- Vars plugins

Plugins will be covered in detail in *Chapter 4*, *Exploring API* and *Chapter 5*, *An In-depth Look at Ansible Plugins*, where you'll learn all you need to know about plugins, including how you can implement them and build your own plugin.

Python API

The Ansible Python API allows you to use Ansible as a library, thus making use of the things that Ansible is good for right from your custom configuration management solution (whatever it is). You can run Ansible playbooks programmatically.

The Python API can also be used from within other Ansible extensions; we'll highlight the important parts throughout this book.

Summary

After going through this chapter, you might be tempted to use Ansible as a configuration management and orchestration tool. Perhaps we have also given you a reason to choose Ansible as an IAC solution. This chapter provided you with a brief introduction to Ansible and its capabilities and use cases. It familiarized you with the Ansible architecture, the different components of Ansible, and the various extension points provided by Ansible. This chapter also took you through the process of contributing to an Ansible project.

In the next chapter, you will be learning about Ansible modules. The chapter will take you through what you need to know before you start writing an Ansible module and guide you through writing your first one. The chapter will also teach you about some best practices that should be followed while developing an Ansible module. Additionally, the chapter will create a base for the more advanced topics that will be covered later in the book, which includes real-life scenarios of where and how you can exploit the power of Ansible.

2
Getting to Know Ansible Modules

Ansible modules are reusable piece of code that can be invoked using the Ansible API or through the Ansible Playbook. Modules form the backbone of Ansible. These are simple pieces of code that can be written in any language.

This chapter will introduce you to writing Ansible modules. The chapter is organized in four sections:

- Writing your first Ansible module
- The module writing helper
- Providing facts
- Testing and debugging modules

Writing your first Ansible module

Ansible modules can be written in any language, though there are a few commandments one needs to abide by while writing them. These are as follows:

- The module must output only valid JSON.
- Modules should be self-contained in one file to be automatically transferred by Ansible.
- Include as few dependencies as possible. If dependencies exist, document them at the top of the module file, and have the module raise the JSON error message when the import fails.

Execution environment

To write your own Ansible module, you first need to understand the execution environment (that is, where and how will your script execute).

Ansible executes the scripts or the play on the target machine. Thus, your script, or the compiled binary, will be copied over to the target machine and then executed. Beware that Ansible simply copies over the module files and generated code for the play on the target machine and makes no attempts to resolve any necessary dependencies. Hence, it is recommended to include as few dependencies as possible in your Ansible module file. Any dependencies in the module need to be properly documented and handled during or before the Ansible play.

Step 1 – module placement

Once you have your module file ready, you need to know exactly where you should place it in order to use the module in the Ansible playbooks.

You can place your module in different places where Ansible looks for modules:

- A path specified by the `library` variable in the configuration file, located at `/etc/ansible/ansible.cfg`
- A path specified by the `–module-path` argument in the command line
- Inside the `library` directory at the root of an Ansible playbook
- Inside the `library` directory of the role, if used

Writing a basic Bash module

Since Ansible modules can be written in any language, we will first try to write one simple Ansible module in Bash.

The first Bash module we will write will simply check for the target machine uptime and return output in JSON, as required by any Ansible module. We will name the module `chkuptime` and write a playbook to execute the same module on the target machine.

This module will be placed in the `library` directory in the root of the Ansible playbook and will be automatically included by Ansible.

The following is a basic Bash module, which checks the uptime of a target machine:

Bash Module Code: (`library/chkuptime`)

```bash
#!/bin/bash

# The module checks for system uptime of the target machine.
# It returns a JSON output since an Ansible module should
# output a Valid JSON.

if [ -f "/proc/uptime" ]; then
    uptime=`cat /proc/uptime`
    uptime=${uptime%%.*}
    days=$(( uptime/60/60/24 ))
    hours=$(( uptime/60/60%24 ))
    uptime="$days days, $hours hours"
else
    uptime=""
fi

echo -e "{\"uptime\":\""$uptime"\"}"
```

For Ansible to include the above module code to be looked up while executing an Ansible playbook, we place it in the `library` directory in the root of the Ansible playbook.

To run this against a target host group, we will create an inventory file named `hosts`, which will include a grouped list of target machines. To test the module, we run it against only one target host.

Now, we will create an Ansible play for executing the newly created module. We name the play `basic_uptime.yml`.

`basic_uptime.yml`

```yaml
---
- hosts: remote
  user: rdas

  tasks:
    - name: Check uptime
      action: chkuptime
      register: uptime

    - debug: var=uptime
```

Directory structure of the playbook:

```
.
├── basic_uptime.yml
├── group_vars
├── hosts
├── library
│   └── chkuptime
└── roles
```

Inventory File (hosts)

```
[remote]
192.168.122.191
```

Now, we run this play, and it should return with the uptime of the target machine:

```
[rdas@localhost ]$ ansible-playbook -i hosts basic_uptime.yml


PLAY [remote] **********************************************************
******


GATHERING FACTS *******************************************************
******
ok: [192.168.122.191]


TASK: [Check uptime] **************************************************
******
ok: [192.168.122.191]


TASK: [debug var=uptime] **********************************************
******
ok: [192.168.122.191] => {
    "var": {
        "uptime": {
            "invocation": {
                "module_args": "",
                "module_name": "chkuptime"
            },
            "uptime": "0 days, 4 hours"
        }
    }
}
```

```
PLAY RECAP *********************************************************
******
192.168.122.191          : ok=3      changed=0     unreachable=0
failed=0
```

Reading arguments

If you notice the above module, it does not accept any arguments. Let's call such a module a `static` module. The module is very limited in its functionality and behavior; otherwise, output cannot be altered. The module will execute on the target machine and return a fixed output. If the user is expecting output in some other form, this module is useless. The module provides no flexibility to the user. For the user to get an output as he or she desires, he or she will either have to search for an alternate of this module (if one exists), or else write one him or herself.

To make a module more flexible, it should be able to respond to the user requirements, modify the output as required, or at least provide ways by which a user can interact with it. This is done by allowing a module to accept arguments. Values to these arguments are specified by the user at runtime.

The arguments, as expected by the module, should be well-defined. The arguments should also be well documented–both for code documentation as well as for generating module documentation. Argument type and default values (if any) should be explicitly defined.

Since a module can be written in any language, there can be different ways in which an Ansible module accepts an argument on the code level. However, passing arguments from the Ansible playbook remains unchanged irrespective of what language the module was written in. In Bash, the arguments are stored in variables with a number in the order of arguments at 1. For example, with a first argument of $1, a second argument would be $2 and so on. However, argument type and default values for the argument need to be handled in the code itself. Ansible provides a Python API, which provides a better way of handling arguments. It allows you to explicitly define the type of argument, mandate an argument, and even specify a default value to the argument. Handling arguments through the Python API will be covered later in this chapter.

We will extend the last module to accept a user argument to print the system uptime in a more detailed format. Using the `detailed` flag, the user may request to print the uptime in full (that is days, hours, minutes, seconds), while the previous format (that is days, hours) is preserved if the `detailed` flag is omitted.

The following is the extension of the chkuptime module, which returns output based on the user-specified value of the detailed flag:

Bash module: (library/chkuptime)

```bash
#!/bin/bash

# The module checks for system uptime of the target machine.
# The module takes in 'detailed' bool argument from the user
# It returns a JSON output since an Ansible module should
# output a Valid JSON.

source $1

if [ -f "/proc/uptime" ]; then
    uptime=`cat /proc/uptime`
    uptime=${uptime%%.*}
    days=$(( uptime/60/60/24 ))
    hours=$(( uptime/60/60%24 ))
    if [ $detailed ]; then
        minutes=$(( uptime/60%60 ))
        seconds=$(( uptime%60 ))
        uptime="$days days, $hours hours, $minutes minutes, $seconds seconds"
    else
        uptime="$days days, $hours hours"
    fi
else
    uptime=""
fi

echo -e "{\"uptime\":\""$uptime"\"}"
```

The only change required in the Ansible play is to pass a Bool type detailed argument to the module when it's called.

Ansible Play (uptime_arg.yml)

```yaml
---
- hosts: remote
  user: rdas

  tasks:
    - name: Check uptime
      action: chkuptime detailed=true
```

```
        register: uptime

  - debug: var=uptime
```

Executing the play, we get the following output:

```
[rdas@localhost bash-arg-example]$ ansible-playbook -i hosts uptime_arg.
yml
PLAY [remote] ********************************************************
******

GATHERING FACTS *****************************************************
******
ok: [192.168.122.191]

TASK: [Check uptime] ************************************************
******
ok: [192.168.122.191]

TASK: [debug var=uptime] ********************************************
******
ok: [192.168.122.191] => {
    "var": {
        "uptime": {
            "invocation": {
                "module_args": "detailed=true",
                "module_name": "chkuptime"
            },
            "uptime": "1 days, 2 hours, 2 minutes, 53 seconds"
        }
    }
}

PLAY RECAP **********************************************************
******
192.168.122.191             : ok=3    changed=0    unreachable=0
failed=0
```

If you compare the output with the previous Ansible play's output, the uptime now includes minutes and seconds, which was missing in the previous example. The previous output can also be achieved by the new module by setting the `detailed` flag as false.

Handling errors

You have already learned how to create a custom module and read user inputs. Since modules are designed to perform some function on the target machine, there are chances it may fail sometimes. Reasons for failure may range from a permission issue on the target machine to invalid user input, or anything else. Whatever the reason may be, your module should be able to handle errors and failures and return an error message with proper information for the user to understand the root cause. All failures should be explicitly reported by including failed in return data.

For instance, let's create a simple module that accepts a process name from the user and returns it whether the specified service is running on the target machine or not. If the service is running, it simply returns a message containing the process ID of the requested process. If not, it explicitly fails the module execution by returning failed as true.

The following is a sample module that includes failed in the return data and explicitly fails the module execution:

Module library/chkprocess

```bash
#!/bin/bash

# This module checks if the pid of the specified
# process exists. If not, it returns a failure msg

source $1

pid=`pidof $process`
if [[ -n $pid ]]; then
    printf '{
        "msg" : "%s is running with pid %s",
        "changed" : 1
    }' "$process" "$pid"
else
    printf '{
        "msg" : "%s process not running",
        "failed" : "True"
    }' "$process"
fi
```

Ansible play chkprocess.yml

```yaml
---
- hosts: remote
  user: rdas

  tasks:
```

```
    - name: Check if process running
      action: chkprocess process=httpd
      register: process

    - debug: msg="{{ process.msg }}"
```

As you can see, we will be checking if the specified `httpd` process is running on the target host. If not, this should fail the Ansible run.

Let's now execute the Ansible play against the target machines:

```
[rdas@localhost process-bash]$ ansible-playbook -i hosts chkprocess.yml
PLAY [remote] ***********************************************************
******

GATHERING FACTS *********************************************************
******
ok: [192.168.122.191]

TASK: [Check if process running] ****************************************
******
failed: [192.168.122.191] => {"failed": "True"}
msg: httpd process not running

FATAL: all hosts have already failed -- aborting

PLAY RECAP **************************************************************
******
          to retry, use: --limit @/home/rdas/chkprocess.retry

192.168.122.191              : ok=1     changed=0     unreachable=0
failed=1
```

As you may notice, since the `httpd` process was not running on the target host, Ansible failed the run as requested. Also, there was a meaningful message displayed in order to inform the user of the root cause of the failure.

Creating Ansible modules in Python

At this point, you are familiar with the basic concepts of writing an Ansible module. We have also gone over some sample Ansible modules that were written in Bash.

While it's possible to write Ansible modules in any language, Ansible provides a friendlier environment for those written in Python.

While writing modules in different languages, as observed above, tasks like handling arguments, handling failures, checking inputs, and so on were handled in the module code itself. In Python, Ansible provides a few helpers and syntactic sugar to perform common tasks. For example, you do not need to parse the arguments as shown in the previous examples.

Common routines provided by Ansible are capable of handling return statuses, errors, failures, and check inputs. This syntactic sugar comes from the AnsibleModule boilerplate. Using the AnsibleModule boilerplate, you can handle arguments and return statuses in a much more efficient way. This will help you concentrate more on the module rather than having to put in explicit checks on inputs.

Let's get a better understanding of the AnsibleModule boilerplate.

The AnsibleModule boilerplate

In order to benefit from the AnsibleModule boilerplate, all you need to do is import `ansible.module_utils.basic`.

Put the import at the end of the file, and make sure your actual module body is contained inside the conventional `main` function.

The AnsibleModule boilerplate also offers a specification language for the module arguments. It allows you to specify if the arguments are optional or required. It also handles a few data types such as enumeration.

In the following code, the module accepts a mandatory argument, `username`, specified by the setting `required=True`:

```
module = AnsibleModule(
    argument_spec = dict(
        username = dict(required=True)
    )
)
username = module.params.get('username')
module.exit_json(changed=True, msg=str(status))
```

The object `module` uses a common function, `exit_json`, which returns `true` and also returns a success message to Ansible. The `module` object provides a set of common functions such as:

- `run_command`: This function runs an external command and gets a return code, `stdout`, `stderr`
- `exit_json`: This function returns a success message to Ansible
- `fail_json`: This function returns a failure and error message to Ansible

Arguments can be accessed by the `module.params` instance variable. There will be a key value pair for each argument.

The `AnsibleModule` helper, while parsing the arguments, will perform a series of validations and requested type conversions. The argument specification dictionary describes each possible argument to the module. An argument can be optional or required. Optional arguments may have a default value. Also, the possible inputs to a particular argument can be restricted using the `choice` keyword.

Documenting modules

If you are writing a module, it is very important to document it properly. Documentation is required for better understanding of what the module does. It is always recommended to document a module.

All you need to do is include a DOCUMENTATION global variable in your module file as shown in the following code. The contents of this variable should be a valid YAML.

```
DOCUMENTATION = """
---
module: chkuser
version_added: 0.1
short_description: Check if user exists on the target machine
options:
    username:
        decription:
            - Accept username from the user
        required: True
"""
```

This documentation can be read using the `ansible-doc` command. Unfortunately, this currently works only for Python-based modules.

In addition to documentation outlining every option in detail, it is a good idea to provide a few examples that may cover some basic use cases for the module. This might be done by adding another global variable named EXAMPLES.

```
EXAMPLES = """
#Usage Example
    - name: Check if user exists
      action: chkuser username=rdas
"""
```

Let's implement the AnsibleModule boilerplate and the preceding documentation in an Ansible module that checks if the user exists on the target machine.

The following is a sample Ansible module, chkuser, built using the AnsibleModule boilerplate. The module also contains module documentation along with usage examples:

Module name: chkuser

```
#!/bin/python

DOCUMENTATION = """
---
module: chkuser
version_added: 0.1
short_description: Check if user exists on the target machine
options:
    username:
        decription:
            - Accept username from the user
        required: True
"""

EXAMPLES = """
#Usage Example
    - name: Check if user exists
      action: chkuser username=rdas
"""

def is_user_exists(username):
    try:
        import pwd
        return(username in [entry.pw_name for entry in pwd.
getpwall()])
    except:
        module.fail_json(msg='Module pwd does not exists')


def main():
```

```
    module = AnsibleModule(
        argument_spec = dict(
            username = dict(required=True)
        )
    )
    username = module.params.get('username')
    exists = is_user_exists(username)
    if exists:
        status = '%s user exists' % username
    else:
        status = '%s user does not exist' % username
    module.exit_json(changed=True, msg=str(status))

from ansible.module_utils.basic import *
main()
```

To use this module, we create an Ansible play, which passes a username as an argument to the `chkuser` module, as shown in the following code:

Ansible Play : `chkuser.yml`

```
---
- hosts: remote
  user: rdas

  tasks:
    - name: Check if user exists
      action: chkuser username=rdas
      register: user

  debug: msg="{{ user.msg }}
```

Executing the play against the target machine returns a message stating whether the queried user exists on the target machine or not.

Testing and debugging modules

Writing modules was easy, but developing a module is not enough. You need to test if the module performs all operations as expected under all circumstances.

It's hard to get something right in the first attempt. Trying out things while you are working on them is a common technique. It's one of the main reasons why dynamic programming and programming environments with short edit and execute cycles have become very popular.

The next section, *Quick local execution*, deals with the problem of running your modules locally, isolated as much as possible from your Ansible environment. This can be of great help during early development and debugging.

Quick local execution

While developing a module, you might want to shorten your edit/run cycle and skip the overhead of actually executing your module through Ansible. As we saw in our previous Bash examples, the execution environment is very simple, and it's pretty straightforward to run the scripts in isolation until you get them right.

However, things get trickier with Python modules using the AnsibleModule boilerplate.

Ansible performs some black magic under the hood of your Python script in order to not require Ansible components to be installed on the target machine. You can explore this technique by employing two simple tricks:

```python
#!/bin/python

import sys

def main():
    module = AnsibleModule(
        argument_spec = dict()
    )
    f = open('/tmp/magicmirror', 'w')
    print >>f, file(sys.argv[0]).read()
    module.exit_json(changed=True)

from ansible.module_utils.basic import *
main()
```

Executing this module locally will generate the file /tmp/magicmirror, which contains code that has been augmented by lining parts of Ansible runtime. It allows you to benefit from shared functionality and avoid introducing dependencies on the target machine.

Another way is to set the environment variable, ANSIBLE_KEEP_REMOTE_FILES=1, on the controller host to prevent Ansible from cleaning up the remote machine by not deleting the generated Ansible scripts, which can then be used for debugging your module.

Best practices

A module can always be improved by following some best practices while they are being developed. This helps in keeping the modules sanitized and easy to understand and extend when required. Some of the best practices which should be followed are:

- The module must be self-contained
- Reduce the dependencies to the minimum
- Write the error cause in the `msg` key
- Try to return only useful output

And don't forget the most important part of developing a module–it should return a valid JSON.

Summary

In this chapter, you learned the basics of writing a module. You grew to understand module placements and things to keep in mind while developing custom modules. You went through writing modules in Bash and moved forward with understanding the AnsibleModule boilerplate, hence ending up developing sample Ansible modules both in Bash and Python. The chapter also covered the best practices that should be followed.

In the next chapter, you will understand error handling and go through a real-life scenario where you can create an Ansible module and exploit the power of Ansible. The next chapter will also cover some complex data structures with Ansible.

3
Digging Deeper into Ansible Modules

Having already learned the basics, this chapter will take you through more advanced topics in Ansible such as:

- Making modules support safe execution in dry run mode
- Understanding how arguments are parsed in an Ansible module
- Handling complex arguments and data structures
- A real life scenario where you can exploit the power of Ansible by creating a custom module to suit your needs

Dry run (check mode)

So, you decided to write your own module which makes a few configuration changes to the system based on the user input. Considering the code has to be run on production, being able to run a simulation of your yet to be published configuration is quite important. Not only is it likely that you'll want to know if your configurations are actually correct before applying them, but you might also want to understand what changes the playbook execution will entail.

Since Ansible does not know the consequences of a module's execution, it just follows instructions from the playbook. In the dry run mode, it will simply print out all the modules it will execute and skip the actual execution. If the module does not support check mode, the module is simply skipped in check mode during execution.

It's useful to show details of any changes a module makes in the state of the system or target machine. However, Ansible can only know that by asking the module to perform a simulation and return with a confirmation on a state change. There may be some tasks in your Ansible playbook that use some modules that return an output. These might be stored in variables, and the following module execution depends on them.

In order to tell Ansible that the module supports check mode and it's safe to run in dry run mode, all that is required is to set a `supports_check_mode` flag to true in the Ansible module. This can be done as follows:

```
module = AnsibleModule(
    argument_spec = dict(
        # List of arguments
    ),
    supports_check_mode = True
)
```

The preceding code in a module enables a module to be executed in dry run mode. You can run your Ansible playbook in check mode using the following command:

ansible-playbook playook.yml --check

This will do a dry run for all the modules that support check mode and report back any changes that would be made on the target machine without actually making the changes.

Loading modules

Before diving into writing Ansible modules, it is necessary to understand how Ansible loads modules during runtime. Understanding how modules are loaded into Ansible allows you to understand the code flow and debug issues that might occur at runtime. To understand this, you must understand how an Ansible playbook is executed.

As you already know, Ansible playbooks are executed using the `ansible-playbook` binary, which accepts a few arguments such as the inventory file and the Ansible play to run. If you take a look at the source code of `ansible-playbook`, you will notice the following import:

```
import ansible.constants as C
```

The `constants.py` file is one of the major files that loads configurations into Ansible. It contains various configurations such as the default path where modules and plugins will be loaded into Ansible.

This file is responsible for defining the order in which the configurations will be loaded by Ansible. The default order in which the configurations are loaded into Ansible is:

1. **ENV**: Environment variables.

2. **CWD**: Current working directory (the directory where the Ansible playbook is executed.

3. **HOME**: Configurations are then loaded from the configuration file in the home directory of the user. This configuration file is named `~/.ansible.cfg`.

4. **Global configuration file**: Ansible places a global configuration file in `/etc/ansible/ansible.cfg`.

Ansible uses the configuration that is found first in the preceding order.

The file also sets in a few default configuration values that are required for Ansible to execute a playbook. Some of these default configuration values are:

- `forks`: The default number of forks is set to 5

- `remote_user`: This is set to active user on the controller node

- `private_key_file`: Sets the default private key to be used to communicate to the target hosts

- `Timeout`: The default value is set to 10

Exploiting Ansible

The previous chapter introduced you to the `AnsibleModule` boilerplate, which allowed you to write your own Ansible modules, accept arguments, and return results. Before moving on to developing an Ansible module, this section will explore the `AnsibleModule` boilerplate in detail from the code level.

Diving deeper into the AnsibleModule boilerplate

The `AnsibleModule` boilerplate, as discussed in the previous chapter, can be used by simply importing `ansible.module_utils.basic` statement.

As soon as you create an object for the `AnsibleModule` class, a few properties are set for the object, including the `argument_spec` property as specified while creating the `AnsibleModule` object. By default, `supports_check_mode` property is set to `false`, and `check_invalid_arguments` is set to `true`.

The `AnsibleModule` class loads the arguments and parameters into the `params` variable using the `load_params` method. The following is the source code for the `load_params` method:

```
def _load_params(self):
    ''' read the input and return a dictionary and the arguments
string '''
    args = MODULE_ARGS
    items   = shlex.split(args)
    params = {}
    for x in items:
        try:
            (k, v) = x.split("=",1)
        except Exception, e:
            self.fail_json(msg="this module requires key=value
arguments (%s)" % (items))
        if k in params:
            self.fail_json(msg="duplicate parameter: %s (value=%s)" %
(k, v))
        params[k] = v
    params2 = json_dict_unicode_to_bytes(json.loads(MODULE_COMPLEX_
ARGS))
    params2.update(params)
    return (params2, args)
```

As you can see, `params` is a dictionary. Python allows you to read values corresponding to a key in a dictionary by using the `get` method. Thus, if you need to access any argument, you can simply use the `get` method on the `params` dictionary variable. This is how Ansible reads and accepts arguments in a module.

Now that you have learned how to develop a module, accept arguments, and handle errors, let's implement this knowledge in a real-life scenario.

So, let's say you have a huge infrastructure at your dispense, which is working great. You have a great configuration management system in place, as well as a monitoring system that keeps a track of all the machines and notifies you in case of failure. Everything is working fine, when one fine day, you need to audit your infrastructure. You need details of each and every machine such as BIOS details, system specifications like manufacturer and serial numbers, and so on.

A simple solution is to run `dmidecode` on each machine and collate the gathered data. Well, running `dmidecode` on individual machines and collating the details is a pain. Let's exploit the power of Ansible to deal with this situation.

Having learned how to create a module, you can use the Python library for dmidecode and write a module of your own, which can then be run on your whole infrastructure. The added advantage is you can have the data in machine parsable form, say JSON, which can later be used to generate reports.

Let's name the module dmidecode and place it in the library directory in the root of the Ansible playbook. The following is the source code for the dmidecode module:

```python
import dmidecode
import json

def get_bios_specs():
    BIOSdict = {}
    BIOSlist = []
    for item in dmidecode.bios().values():
        if type(item) == dict and item['dmi_type'] == 0:
            BIOSdict["Name"] = str((item['data']['Vendor']))
            BIOSdict["Description"] = str((item['data']['Vendor']))
            BIOSdict["BuildNumber"] = str((item['data']['Version']))
            BIOSdict["SoftwareElementID"] = str((item['data']['BIOS Revision']))
            BIOSdict["primaryBIOS"] = "True"
            BIOSlist.append(BIOSdict)
    return BIOSlist


def get_proc_specs():
    PROCdict = {}
    PROClist = []
    for item in dmidecode.processor().values():
        if type(item) == dict and item['dmi_type'] == 4:
            PROCdict['Vendor'] = str(item['data']['Manufacturer']['Vendor'])
            PROCdict['Version'] = str(item['data']['Version'])
            PROCdict['Thread Count'] = str(item['data']['Thread Count'])
            PROCdict['Characteristics'] = str(item['data']['Characteristics'])
            PROCdict['Core Count'] = str(item['data']['Core Count'])
            PROClist.append(PROCdict)
    return PROClist


def get_system_specs():
```

```
        SYSdict = {}
        SYSlist = []
        for item in dmidecode.system().values():
            if item['dmi_type'] == 1:
                SYSdict['Manufacturer'] = str(item['data']
['Manufacturer'])
                SYSdict['Family'] = str(item['data']['Family'])
                SYSdict['Serial Number'] = str(item['data']['Serial
Number'])
                SYSlist.append(SYSdict)
        return SYSlist


def main():
    module = AnsibleModule(
        argument_spec = dict(
            save = dict(required=False, default=False, type='bool'),
        )
    )
    # You can record all data you want. For demonstration purpose, the
#example records only the first record.
    dmi_data = json.dumps({
        'Hardware Specs' : {
            'BIOS' : get_bios_specs()[0],
            'Processor' : get_proc_specs()[0],
            'System' : get_system_specs()[0]
        }
    })
    save = module.params.get('save')
    if save:
        with open('dmidecode.json', 'w') as dfile:
            dfile.write(str(dmi_data))
    module.exit_json(changed=True, msg=str(dmi_data))


from ansible.module_utils.basic import *
main()
```

As you can see, we are collecting data such as processor specs, BIOS specs, and system specs; you can always extend the module based on your personal needs.

The module accepts a Boolean argument, save, from the user, which, if set to true, will write the result to a JSON file on the remote machine.

You may notice that the module has an import line, `import dmidecode`, at the beginning. The statement imports the `dmidecode` Python library. The library is provided by the `python-dmidecode` package. Since the module depends on the `dmidecode` Python library, this is required to be installed on the target machine. This can be handled in the Ansible playbook.

Dependencies can be specified in the `global_vars` file and can be used by the variable name in the Ansible playbook. This is done to prevent making changes to the Ansible play in case there is a change in the dependency. This can be specified in the `global_vars` directory as follows:

```
global_vars/all

    # Dependencies
    dependencies:
        - python-dmidecode
        - python-simplejson
```

So, the Ansible module is ready and the dependencies are taken care of. You will now have to create the Ansible play, which will execute the `dmidecode` module on the target machines. Let's name the Ansible `play dmidecode.yml`.

```
    ---
    - hosts: remote
      user: root

      tasks:
        - name: Install dependencies
          yum: name={{ item }} state=latest
          with_items:
            - "{{ dependencies }}"

        - name: Test dmidecode
          action: dmidecode save=True
          register: dmi_data

        - debug: var=dmi_data['msg']
```

Executing the Ansible playbook will run the `dmidecode` module on the remote host group. Since `save` is set to `true`, this will create a `dmidecode.json` file on the remote host containing the required information.

Complex arguments

Since the Ansible module is just another code that can accept and parse arguments, there might be a question of whether it's capable of handling complex variable sets. Although Ansible is used as a deployment, orchestration, and configuration management tool, it is designed to handle simple arguments, and it is still capable of handling complex variables. This is an advanced topic, and since this is not generally used, this section will cover it in brief.

You have already learned how to pass arguments to an Ansible module. However, complex arguments are handled differently.

Reading complex arguments

Let's take an example of the complex variable, `complex_var`, which, as usual, we define in `group_vars/all`:

```
# Complex Variable
complex_var:
    key0: value0
    key1:
      - value1
      - value2
```

The preceding variable is of the dictionary type (that is a key value pair). For an Ansible module to parse this kind of argument, we need to make a few changes in the way complex variables are passed in the module and the way they are parsed. We write a custom module that accepts this complex variable as an argument and prints the values for the associated keys. We name the module `complex`.

The following is the code for the `complex.py` module:

Ansible Module: `library/complex.py`

```python
#!/usr/bin/python

def main():
    module = AnsibleModule(
        argument_spec = dict(
            key0 = dict(required=True),
            key1 = dict(required=False, default=[])
        )
    )
    module.exit_json(changed=False, out='%s, %s' %
```

```
        (module.params['key0'], module.params['key1']))

    from ansible.module_utils.basic import *
    main()
```

The preceding module accepts the complex variable and prints their associated values for the respective keys. The way complex variables are passed to the Ansible module is specified in the Ansible play.

The following is the Ansible playbook, which takes in complex arguments and passes them on to the complex module:

Ansible play: `complex.yaml`

```
    ---
    - hosts: localhost
      user: rdas

      tasks:
        - name: print complex variable key values
          action: complex
          args: '{{ complex_var }}'
          register: res

        - debug: msg='{{res.out}}'
```

The Ansible playbook, when executed, prints the values associated with the keys `key0` and `key1`, respectively.

Summary

In this chapter, you learned about making your module support dry runs by introducing the `supports_check_mode` flag. You also learned how arguments are handled in Ansible. The chapter covered a real-life scenario where a custom Ansible module was used to perform a hardware audit on the infrastructure. The chapter also covered in brief how complex variables are handled with Ansible.

In the next chapter, you will learn about Ansible plugins, why are they needed, and how they fit in the general Ansible structure. The chapter will also cover the Python plugin API.

4
Exploring API

Ansible plugins are an advanced topic. There are various plugins available for Ansible. This chapter will cover different Python API and lookup plugins in brief and explore how they fit into the general Ansible architecture.

Ansible is pluggable in a lot of ways. It is possible that there are components of business logic that don't quite fit in. Hence, Ansible provides extension points that can be used to fit your business needs. Ansible plugins are another such extension point where you can build your own plugins to extend Ansible to address your business logic.

Python API

Before exploring plugins, it's important to understand the Ansible Python API. The Ansible Python API can be used for the following:

- To control the nodes
- To respond to the various Python events
- To write various plugins as per the requirement
- Inventory data from various external data stores can also be plugged in

Python API for Ansible allows Ansible to run programmatically. Running Ansible programmatically through the Python API has the following advantages:

- **Better error handling**: Since everything is Python, it becomes easy to handle errors as and when they occur. This gives more control and confidence in the code by providing a better context in case of errors.
- **Extending Ansible**: One of the drawbacks, as you might have noticed in the previous runs, is that, by default, Ansible simply writes the output on `stdout` and does not log anything to a file. To address this, you can write your own custom plugins to save output to a file or database for future reference.

- **Unknown variables**: There may be cases where complete knowledge of the required variables may be discovered only during runtime, for example, when an IP of an instance launched on the cloud during the Ansible play. Running Ansible programmatically using the Python API can address this issue.

Now that you know the advantages of using Python API for Ansible, let's explore the Python API and take a look at how one can interact with Ansible through the API.

This chapter will cover the three most important classes that are used extensively:

- **Runner**: Used to execute individual modules
- **Playbook**: Helps in executing the Ansible playbook
- **Callbacks**: Gets back the run results on the controller node

Let's take an in-depth look at what these classes are and explore the various extension points.

Runner

The `runner` class is the core API interface of Ansible. The `runner` class is used to execute individual modules. If there is one single module that needs to be executed, for example, the `setup` module, we can use the `runner` class to execute this module.

 One can have multiple `runner` objects in the same Python file to run different modules.

Let's explore a sample code, where the `runner` class will be used to execute the `setup` module on localhost. This will print a lot of details about localhost such as time, operating system (distribution), IP, Netmask, and hardware details such as architecture, free memory, used memory, machine ID, and so on.

```
from ansible import runner

runner = runner.Runner(
    module_name = 'setup',
    transport = 'local'
)

print runner.run()
```

This will execute the `setup` module on localhost. This is equivalent to running the following command:

```
ansible all -i "localhost," -c local -m setup
```

To run the preceding module on remote machines or a group of machines, one can specify hosts in an inventory that can later be passed as an argument in the `runner` object, along with a remote user that should be used to log into the remote machine. You can also specify a pattern of hosts, specifically on which the module needs to be executed. This is done by passing the pattern argument to the `runner` object.

> You can also pass in a module argument using the `module_args` key.

For instance, if you need to get memory details of remote machines that have their domain names set as `store1.mytestlab.com`, `store2.mytestlab.com`, `store12.mytestlab.com`, and so on, this can be simply achieved in the following manner:

```
from ansible import runner

runner = runner.Runner(
    module_name = 'setup',
    pattern = 'store*',
    module_args = 'filter=ansible_memory_mb'
)

print runner.run()
```

The preceding code will execute the `setup` module on all twelve hosts and print the memory status that is reachable by each host. Reachable hosts will be listed under "contacted," while those that are un-reachable will be listed under "dark."

Apart from the arguments discussed above, the `runner` class provides a large number of interfacing options through the arguments that it accepts. The following is a list of a few arguments as defined in the source code, along with their use:

Arguments/default values	Description
`host_list=C.DEFAULT_HOST_LIST`	Example: `/etc/ansible/hosts`, legacy usage
`module_path=None`	Example: `/usr/share/ansible`
`module_name=C.DEFAULT_MODULE_NAME`	Example: `copy`
`module_args=C.DEFAULT_MODULE_ARGS`	Example: `"src=/tmp/a dest=/tmp/b"`
`forks=C.DEFAULT_FORKS`	Parallelism level
`timeout=C.DEFAULT_TIMEOUT`	SSH timeout
`pattern=C.DEFAULT_PATTERN`	Which hosts? Example: "all" `acme.example.org`

Arguments/default values	Description
`remote_user=C.DEFAULT_REMOTE_USER`	Example: "username"
`remote_pass=C.DEFAULT_REMOTE_PASS`	Example: "password123" or "None" if using key
`remote_port=None`	If SSH on different ports
`private_key_file=C.DEFAULT_PRIVATE_KEY_FILE`	If not using keys/passwords
`transport=C.DEFAULT_TRANSPORT`	"SSH," "paramiko," "Local"
`conditional=True`	Run only if this fact expression evals to `true`
`callbacks=None`	Used for output
`sudo=False`	Whether to run sudo or not
`inventory=None`	Reference to inventory object
`environment=None`	Environment variables (as `dict`) to use inside the command
`complex_args=None`	Structured data in addition to `module_args`, must be a `dict`

Playbook

Playbook, as you have learned in the previous chapters, is a set of instructions or commands in a YAML format that runs in a sequential order. Python API for Ansible provides a rich interface to run the already created playbooks through the `PlayBook` class.

You can create a `PlayBook` object and pass in an existing Ansible playbook as an argument along with the required parameters. One thing to note is that multiple plays do not execute simultaneously, but the tasks in a play can be executed in parallel based on the requested number of forks. Once the object is created, you can easily execute the Ansible playbook by calling the `run` function.

You can create a `Playbook` object that can later be executed using the following template:

```
pb = PlayBook(
    playbook = '/path/to/playbook.yaml',
    host_list = '/path/to/inventory/file',
    stats = 'object/of/AggregateStats',
    callbacks = 'playbookCallbacks object',
    runner_callbacks = 'callbacks/used/for/Runner()'
)
```

One thing to note here is that a `PlayBook` object requires at least four mandatory arguments to be passed. These are:

- `playbook`: the path to a Playbook file
- `stats`: Holds aggregated data about events occurring in each host
- `callbacks`: Outputs callbacks for the playbook
- `runner_callbacks`: Callbacks for the `runner` API

You can also define the verbosity in a range of `0-4`, which is required by the `callbacks` and `runner_callbacks` objects. If verbosity is not defined, the default value is taken as `0`. Defining verbosity as a `4` is equivalent to using `-vvvv` while executing the Ansible playbook from the command line.

For instance, you have your inventory file named `hosts` and a playbook named `webservers.yaml`. To execute this playbook on the inventory hosts using the Python API, you need to create a `PlayBook` object with the required parameters. You also need to require a verbose output. This can be done as follows:

```
from ansible.playbook import PlayBook
from ansible import callbacks
VERBOSITY = 4
pb = PlayBook(
    playbook = 'webservers.yaml',
    host_list = 'hosts',
    stats = callbacks.AggregateStats(),
    callbacks = callbacks.PlaybookCallbacks(verbose=VERBOSITY),
    runner_callbacks = callbacks.PlaybookRunnerCallbacks(
                    callbacks.AggregateStats(),
                    verbose=VERBOSITY)
)

pb.run()
```

This will execute the playbook `webservers.yaml` on the remote hosts specified in the `hosts` inventory file.

To execute the same playbook locally, just as you did in the `runner` object earlier, you need to pass the argument `transport=local` in the `PlayBook` object and remove the `host_list` argument.

Apart from the discussed parameters, PlayBook accepts a whole lot more.

The following is a list of all the arguments accepted by the `PlayBook` object along with their purpose:

Argument	Description
playbook	Path to a playbook file
host_list	Path to a file like /etc/ansible/hosts
module_path	Path to Ansible modules, like /usr/share/ansible/
forks	Desired level of parallelism
timeout	Connection timeout
remote_user	Run as this user if not specified in a particular play
remote_pass	Use this remote password (for all plays) vs using SSH keys
sudo_pass	If sudo=true and a password is required, this is the sudo password
remote_port	Default remote port to use if not specified with the host or play
transport	How to connect to hosts that don't specify a transport (local, paramiko, and so on.)
callbacks	Output callbacks for the playbook
runner_callbacks	More callbacks, this time for the runner API
stats	Holds aggregate data about events occurring to each host
sudo	If not specified per play, requests all plays use sudo mode
inventory	Can be specified instead of host_list to use a pre-existing inventory object
check	Don't change anything; just try to detect some potential changes
any_errors_fatal	Terminate the entire execution immediately when one of the hosts has failed
force_handlers	Continue to notify and run handlers even if a task fails

Callbacks

Ansible provides hooks for running custom callbacks on the host machine as it invokes various modules. Callbacks allow us to log the events and operations that are started or completed and aggregate results from the module execution. Python API provides callbacks for this purpose, which can be used in its default state as well as to develop your own callback plugins.

Callbacks allow various operations to be performed. Callbacks can also be exploited as an extension point for Ansible. Some of the most widely used callbacks operations while wrapping up Ansible in Python API are:

- `AggregateStats`: As the name suggests, `AggregateStats` holds the aggregated stats surrounding per host activity during a playbook run. An object of `AggregateStats` can be passed on as an argument for `stats` in the `PlayBook` object.

- `PlaybookRunnerCallbacks`: An object of `PlaybookRunnerCallbacks` is used for `Runner()`, for example, when a single module is executed using the `Runner` API interface, `PlaybookRunnerCallbacks` is used to return the task status.

- `PlaybookCallbacks`: An object of `PlaybookCallbacks` is used by the playbook API interface of the Python API when a playbook is executed from the Python API. These callbacks are used by `/usr/bin/ansible-playbook`.

- `DefaultRunnerCallbacks`: When there are no callbacks specified for `Runner` to use, `DefaultRunnerCallbacks` is used.

- `CliRunnerCallbacks`: This extends `DefaultRunnerCallbacks` and overrides the on-event trigger functions, basically optimized to be used with `/usr/bin/ansible`.

Ansible plugins

Plugins are another extension point that haven't yet been touched on in this book. Also, there is very limited documentation available, even on the Internet, regarding plugins.

Plugins are an advanced topic that will be covered in the next chapter. However, it's important to understand the Python API behind plugins in order to understand how plugins work and how they can be extended.

PluginLoader

As the code documentation states, `PluginLoader` is the base class that loads plugins from the configured plugin directories. It iterates through the list of play basedirs, configured paths, and Python paths to search for a plugin. The first match is used.

An object of `PluginLoader` takes in the following arguments:

- `class_name`: The specific class name for plugin type
- `required_base_class`: The base class required by the plugin module
- `package`: Package information
- `config`: Specifies the default path from configuration
- `subdir`: All subdirectories in a package
- `aliases`: Alternate name for the plugin type

For every Ansible plugin, there is a defined class name that needs to be used. This class in `PluginLoader` is identified by `required_base_class`. The different categories of Ansible plugins along with their base names are listed in the following table:

Plugin type	Class name
Action plugins	`ActionModule`
Cache plugins	`CacheModule`
Callback plugins	`CallbackModule`
Connection plugins	`Connection`
Shell plugins	`ShellModule`
Lookup plugins	`LookupModule`
Vars plugins	`VarsModule`
Filter plugins	`FilterModule`
Test plugins	`TestModule`
Strategy plugins	`StrategyModule`

Summary

This chapter took you through the Python API for Ansible and introduced you to more advanced ways of using Ansible. This included executing single tasks without creating an entire playbook to executing a playbook programmatically.

This chapter also introduced you to the various components of the Ansible Python API from a more technical point of view, exploring the various extension points and ways to exploit them.

This chapter additionally sets a base for the next chapter, which will be a deep dive into the Ansible plugins. The next chapter will utilize the knowledge gained from this chapter to create custom Ansible plugins. We will explore different Ansible plugins and guide you through writing your own Ansible plugin in the following chapter.

5
An In-Depth Look at Ansible Plugins

The previous chapter introduced you to the Python API and various extension points provided by Ansible. By the time you reach this chapter, you should already know how a plugin is loaded by Ansible. The previous chapter listed the different types of Ansible plugins.

This chapter is a deep dive into what Ansible plugins are and how you can write your own custom Ansible plugin. In this chapter, we will discuss the different types of Ansible plugins in detail and explore them on a code level. Together, we will walk through the Ansible Python API, and you will use the extension points to write your own Ansible plugins.

As discussed in the previous chapter, the plugins are categorized as follows:

- Lookup plugins
- Action plugins
- Cache plugins
- Callback plugins
- Connection plugins
- Var plugins
- Filter plugins

Out of these plugins, the most commonly used are lookup plugins, callback plugins, var plugins, filter plugins, and connection plugins. Let's explore the plugins one by one.

Lookup plugins

Lookup plugins are designed to read data from different sources and feed them to Ansible. The data source can be either the local file system on the controller node or from an external data source. These may also be for file formats that are not natively supported by Ansible.

If you decide to write your own lookup plugin, you need to drop it in one of the following directories for Ansible to pick it up during the execution of an Ansible playbook.

- The directory named `lookup_plugins` in the project `Root`
- In `~/.ansible/plugins/lookup_plugins/` or
- `/usr/share/ansible_plugins/lookup_plugins/`

By default, a number of lookup plugins are already available in Ansible. Let's discuss some of the most commonly used lookup plugins.

Lookup pluginfile

This is the most basic type of lookup plugin available in Ansible. It reads through a file's content on the controller node. The data read from the file can then be fed to the Ansible playbook as a variable. In its most basic form, usage of a file lookup is demonstrated in the following Ansible playbook:

```
---
- hosts: all
  vars:
    data: "{{ lookup('file', './test-file.txt') }}"
  tasks:
- debug: msg="File contents {{ data }}"
```

The preceding playbook will read data off a local file, `test-file.txt`, from the playbook root directory into the variable `data`. This variable is then fed to the `task:` `debug` module and uses the data variable to print it on screen.

Lookup plugin – csvfile

The `csvfile` lookup plugin was designed to read data from a CSV file on the controller node. This lookup module is designed to take in several parameters, which are discussed as follows:

Parameter	Default value	Description
file	ansible.csv	File to read data from.
delimiter	TAB	Delimiter used in CSV file. Usually ','.
col	1	Column number (index).
default	Empty string	Returns this value if the requested key is not found in the CSV file

Let's take an example of reading data from the following CSV file. The CSV file contains population and area details of different cities:

```
File: city-data.csv
City, Area, Population
Pune, 700, 2.5 Million
Bangalore, 741, 4.3 Million
Mumbai, 603, 12 Million
```

This file lies in the controller node at the root of the Ansible play. To read off data from this file, the csvfile lookup plugin is used. The following Ansible play tries to read the population of Mumbai from the preceding CSV file.

Ansible Play : test-csv.yaml

```
---
- hosts: all
  tasks:
    - debug:
        msg="Population of Mumbai is {{lookup('csvfile', 'Mumbai
file=city-data.csv delimiter=, col=2')}}"
```

Lookup plugin – dig

The dig lookup plugin can be used to run DNS queries against a **FQDN (Fully Qualified Domain Name)**. You can customize the lookup plugin's output by using the different flags that are supported by the plugin. In its most basic form, it returns the IP of the given FQDN.

This plugin has a dependency on the python-dns package. This should be installed on the controller node.

The following Ansible play explains how to fetch the TXT records for any FQDN:

```
---
- hosts: all
  tasks:
    - debug: msg="TXT record {{ lookup('dig', 'yahoo.com./TXT') }}"
    - debug: msg="IP of yahoo.com {{lookup('dig', 'yahoo.com',
wantlist=True)}}"
```

The preceding Ansible play will fetch the TXT records in step one and any IPs associated with the FQDN `yahoo.com` in step two.

It is also possible to perform reverse DNS lookups with the dig plugin by using the following syntax:

```
- debug: msg="Reverse DNS for 8.8.8.8 is {{ lookup('dig', '8.8.8.8/PTR')
}}"
```

Lookup plugin – ini

The `ini` lookup plugin is designed to read data off a `.ini` file. The `ini` file in general is a collection of key-value pairs under defined sections. The `ini` lookup plugin supports the following parameters:

Parameter	Default value	Description
type	ini	Type of file. Currently supports two formats–ini and property.
file	ansible.ini	Name of file to read data from.
section	global	Section of the `ini` file from which the specified key needs to be read from.
re	False	If the key is a regular expression, set this to `true`.
default	Empty string	If the requested key is not found in the `ini` file, return this.

Taking an example of the following `ini` file, let's try to read some keys using the `ini` lookup plugin. The file is named `network.ini`:

```
[default]
bind_host = 0.0.0.0
bind_port = 9696
log_dir = /var/log/network

[plugins]
core_plugin = rdas-net
firewall = yes
```

The following Ansible play will read off the keys from the `ini` file:

```
---
- hosts: all
  tasks:
```

```
      - debug: msg="core plugin {{ lookup('ini', 'core_plugin
file=network.ini section=plugins') }}"
      - debug: msg="core plugin {{ lookup('ini', 'bind_port
file=network.ini section=default') }}"
```

The `ini` lookup plugin can also be used to read off values through a file that does not contain sections, for instance, a Java property file.

Loops – lookup plugins for iteration

There are times when you may need to perform the same task over and over again. It might be the case of installing various dependencies for a package or multiple inputs that go through the same operation, for instance, checking and starting various services. Just like any other programming language provides a way to iterate over data to perform repetitive tasks, Ansible also provides a clean way to carry out the same operation. The concept is called looping and is provided by Ansible lookup plugins.

Loops in Ansible are generally identified as those starting with `with_`. Ansible supports a number of looping options. Few of the most commonly used are discussed in the following sections.

Standard loop – with_items

This is the simplest and most commonly used loop in Ansible. It is used to iterate over an item list and perform some operation on it. The following Ansible play demonstrates the use of the `with_items` lookup loop:

```
---
- hosts: all
  tasks:
    - name: Install packages
      yum: name={{ item }} state=present
      with_items:
        - vim
        - wget
        - ipython
```

The `with_items` loop supports the use of hashes where you can access the variables by using the item <keyname> in the Ansible playbook. The following playbook demonstrates the use of `with_items` to iterate over a given hash:

```
---
- hosts: all
  tasks:
    - name: Create directories with specific permissions
```

```
file: path={{item.dir}} state=directory mode={{item.mode | int}}
with_items:
  - { dir: '/tmp/ansible', mode: 755 }
  - { dir: '/tmp/rdas', mode: 755 }
```

The preceding playbook will create two directories with the specified permission sets. If you look closely while accessing the mode key from item, there exists a block of code named | int. This is a jinja2 filter, which is used to convert a string to an integer.

Do until loop–until

This loop has the same implementation as that of any other programming language. It executes at least once and keeps executing unless a specific condition is reached.

Lets take a look at the following code to understand the do-until loop:

```
- name: Clean up old file. Keep only the latest 5
  action: shell /tmp/clean-files.sh
  register: number
  until: number.stdout.find('5') != -1
  retries: 6
  delay: 10
```

The clean-files.sh script performs a cleanup operation on the specified directory and keeps only the latest five files. On every execution, it removes the oldest file and returns the number of files remaining in the directory being cleaned up as output on stdout. The script looks something like this:

```
#!/bin/bash

DIR_CLEAN='/tmp/test'
cd $DIR_CLEAN
OFNAME=`ls -t | tail -1`
rm -f $OFNAME
COUNT=`ls | wc -w`
echo $COUNT
```

This operation will be retried a maximum of six times, with a delay of 10. The loop exists once it finds a 5 in the number register variable.

If "retries" and "delay" are not specified explicitly, a task in such cases, by default, is retried three times with a delay of five.

Create your own lookup plugin

The previous chapter introduced you to the Python API and explained how various plugins are loaded by Ansible to be used in the Ansible play. This chapter covers some already available Ansible lookup plugins and explains how those can be used. This section will try to replicate a functionality of the dig lookup to get the IP address of a given FQDN. This will be done without using the dnspython library and will use the basic socket library for Python. The following example is only a demonstration of how you can write your own Ansible lookup plugin:

```python
import socket

class LookupModule(object):

    def __init__(self, basedir=None, **kwargs):
        self.basedir = basedir

    def run(self, hostname, inject=None, **kwargs):
        hostname = str(hostname)
        try:
            host_detail = socket.gethostbyname(hostname)
        except:
            host_detail = 'Invalid Hostname'
        return host_detail
```

The preceding code is a lookup plugin; let's call it hostip.

As you can see, there exists a class named LookupModule. Ansible identifies a Python file or module as a lookup plugin only when there is a class called LookupModule. The module takes in an argument hostname and checks if there exists an IP corresponding to it (that is, if it can be resolved to a valid IP address). If yes, it returns the IP address of the requested FQDN. If not, it returns Invalid Hostname.

To use this module, place it in the lookup_modules directory at the root of the Ansible play. The following playbook demonstrates how you can use the newly created hostip lookup:

```yaml
---

- hosts: all
  tasks:
    - debug:
        msg="{{lookup('hostip', item, wantlist=True)}}"
      with_items:
        - www.google.co.in
        - saliux.wordpress.com
        - www.twitter.com
```

The preceding play will loop through the list of websites and pass it as an argument to the `hostip` lookup plugin. This will in turn return the IP associated with the requested domain. You may have noticed that, there is an argument called `wantlist=True` that is also passed in while the `hostip` lookup plugin is called. This is to handle multiple outputs (that is, if there are multiple values associated with the requested domain, the values will be returned as a list). This makes it easy to iterate over the output values.

Callback plugins

Callbacks are one of the most widely used plugins with Ansible. They allow you to respond back to the events of an Ansible run during runtime. Callbacks are a type of plugin that is customized the most.

Though there are a few generic callback plugins, you most certainly may end up writing one yourself to address your requirements. This is because everyone has a different perception of what they want to do with the data. Ansible is not just a tool limited to configuration management and orchestration. You can do much more, for instance, collect data during the Ansible plays and process them later on. Callbacks provide a vast playground with possibilities to explore. It's all about what you want to do with the results.

This section, rather than going through the existing callback modules, will focus more on writing one.

Taking a scenario from previous chapters, you created your own `dmidecode` module, which executed on the target machines and returned a JSON of hardware specs. The module also supported a flag that allowed you to store this result in a JSON file on the target machine itself.

Looking at the scenario, there are two major concerns:

- You don't have a log of playbook execution. Everything is on `stdout`.
- Even if you set the save flag to true while calling the `dmidecode` module, the results are stored on the target machine and not on the controller node. Post playbook execution, you'll have to collect these JSON files individually from each target host.

The first point is an issue you never want in your production environment. You always want to have logs of the Ansible play. This will allow you to later trace back any failures that occurred during the playbook execution. There are a few generic callback plugins already available in the Ansible code repository for this purpose. The link `https://github.com/ansible/ansible/tree/devel/lib/ansible/plugins/callback` is where you can find some of the existing callback modules. You may choose one of them if they satisfy your needs. This section will not discuss the existing callback modules.

The second point is a major reason why people choose to develop their own callback plugins. It addresses the concern of what you actually want to do with the data. In this particular case, the module collects system information, which can come in handy later for audit purposes. In other cases, you might still want to process the collected information and logs of the Ansible play in order to determine cause of failure, generate reports, keep a track of production changes, and so on. There can be a number of possibilities.

This section will address the second point by creating a custom callback plugin that can help you get back the JSON data from the target machine, which was generated by using the `dmidecode` module that you created in *Chapter 3, Digging Deeper into Ansible Modules*.

Before diving into writing a callback module, it's important to know how a callback module works.

A callback module works on events that occur during a playbook execution. The various commonly used events as supported in Ansible are:

- `runner_on_failed`
- `runner_on_ok`
- `runner_on_skipped`
- `runner_on_unreachable`
- `runner_on_no_hosts`
- `playbook_on_start`

Events that have a name starting with `runner_` are specific to tasks. Events that have names starting with `playbook_` are specific to the entire playbook. Clearly, event names are self-explanatory; hence, we will not be going into detail of what every event means.

As described in the previous chapter, the callback plugin should have a class named `CallbackModule`, without which Ansible will not identify it as a callback plugin. Python API requires the `CallbackModule` class to identify a module as a callback plugin. This is required to differentiate between different Python files, as different Python modules may reside in the same directory and the callback plugin might be using methods from one of the Python modules in the same directory.

Having discussed the events and class requirements, it's time to get our hands dirty. Let's move on to writing a very basic callback plugin that integrates with the `dmidecode` module created in *Chapter 3, Digging Deeper into Ansible Modules*.

If you remember, the Ansible play recorded the JSON output in a register named `dmi_data`. This data was then echoed on `stdout` by means of the debug module. The callback module thus needs to look for the `dmi_data` key during the playbook execution. This key will contain the output JSON. The callback plugin will attempt to dump this JSON data in a JSON file on the controller node and name it as either the target machine's IP or FQDN followed by the `.json` extension. The callback module is named `logvar` and needs to be placed in the `callback_plugins` directory at the root of the Ansible play.

```
import json

class CallbackModule(object):

    '''
    This logs the debug variable 'var' and writes it in a JSON file
    '''

    def runner_on_ok(self, host, result):
        try:
            if result['var']['dmi_data[\'msg\']']:
                fname = '%s.json' % host
                with open(fname, 'w') as ofile:
                    json.dump(result['var']['dmi_data[\'msg\']'],
ofile)
        except:
            pass
```

Executing the `dmidecode` playbook after placing the above module in the `callback_plugins` directory in the root of Ansible play will result in output files named `<taget>.json`. These files contain the `dmidecode` information of the target machine as returned by the `dmidecode` module.

Var plugins

While writing an Ansible play, you most certainly will use some variables. It might be the host-specific `host_vars` or the commonly used `group_vars`. Any data that is read from these and fed to the Ansible playbook is done using the var plugins.

The var plugin is identified by the classname `VarModule`. If you explore the var plugin on a code level, inside the class, there are three methods:

- `run`: This method should return both the host-specific vars as well as vars calculated from groups it is a member of
- `get_host_vars`: Returns host-specific variables
- `get_group_vars`: Returns group-specific variables

Connection plugins

Connection plugins define how Ansible connects to the remote machine. Ansible can be used to perform operations on various platforms by means of defining playbooks. Hence, for different platforms, you may require different connection plugins to be used.

By default, Ansible ships with `paramiko_ssh`, native SSH, and a local connection plugin. Support for a docker has also been added. There are other less known, less used connection plugins, too, like chroot, jail zone, and libvirt.

A connection plugin is identified by its class connection.

Let's explore the Paramiko connection plugin on a code level. The connection class contains four major methods. These in turn call a few private functions for a few operations. The major methods are:

- `exec_command`: This method runs the requested command on the remote target. You may have a requirement to run commands using `sudo`, which requires a PTY by default. Paramiko handles this by passing `pty=True` by default.

- `put_file`: This method takes in two parameters – the `in_path` and `out_path`. This function is used to copy over files from the local controller node to the remote target machine.

- `fetch_file`: This method, similar to the `put_file` method, also takes in two parameters – the `in_path` and `out_path`. The method is used to fetch files from the remote machine to the local controller node.

- `Close`: This function terminates the connection when the operation is complete.

Filter plugin

Ansible supports Jinja2 templating, but why not Jinja2 filters? You want it; Ansible has it!

Filter plugins are Jinja2 template filters that can be used to modify or transform the template expression from one form to another. Ansible already has a set of Jinja2 filters that come by default. For instance, `to_yaml` and `to_json`. Ansible also supports reading data from already formatted texts. For instance, if you already have a YAML file or a JSON file from which you need to read data, you can use the `from_json` or `from_yaml` filter.

You can also choose to convert a string to an integer by using the int filter, as demonstrated in the *Loops – lookup plugins for iteration* section while creating directories with defined permissions.

Let's discuss how and where the filters can be implemented to get even more out of Ansible.

Using filters with conditions

While running a script, a situation might occur where, based on the outcome of the previous step, you need to perform a particular step. This is where conditions come into the picture. In normal programming, you can use the if-else conditional statement. In Ansible, you need to check the output of the last command and apply a filter along with the when clause, as shown in the following code:

```
---
- hosts: all
  tasks:
    - name: Run the shell script
      shell: /tmp/test.sh
      register: output

    - name: Print status
    - debug: msg="Success"
      when: output|success

    - name: Print status
    - debug: msg="Failed"
      when: output|failed
```

In the preceding script, the result of the execution of the shell script test.sh is stored in the register variable output. If the status is a success, the task will print Success; otherwise, it will print Failed.

Version comparison

This filter can be used to check which version of the requested application is installed on the target host. It returns a True or False status. The version comparison filter accepts the following operators:

```
<, lt, <=, le, >, gt, >=, ge, ==, =, eq, !=, <>, ne
```

IP address filter

The IP address filter can be used to check if the provided string is a valid IP address or not. You can even specify what protocol you are checking against: IPv4 or Ipv6.

The following filter will check if the IP address is a valid Ipv4 address:

```
{{ host_ip | ipv4 }}
```

In the same way, an IP address can be checked to see if it's a valid Ipv6 address or not by using:

```
{{ host_ip | ipv6 }}
```

Understanding the code

A Python module is identified by Ansible as a filter plugin by looking for a class named `FilterModule`. Inside this class there exists one method named `filters`, which maps the filters to their corresponding file outside the `FilterModule` class.

The following is a structure of the filter plugin if you choose to write one yourself:

```
# Import dependencies

def custom_filter(**kwargs):
    # filter operation code

class FilterModule(object):
    def filter(self):
        return {
            'custom_filter': custom_filter
        }
```

In the preceding sample code, in the filter method inside the `FilterModule` class, the `custom_filter` key maps to the `custom_filter` function outside the class.

The `custom_filter` function contains the actual filter implementation code. Ansible simply loads the `FilterModule` class and reads through the defined filters. The defined filters are then made available to the end user.

In the Ansible code base, any new suggestions for filters are normally added to the `core.py` file inside the filter plugins.

Summary

This chapter continued where *Chapter 4, Exploring API* ended and picked up on how the Ansible Python API for plugins is implemented in the various Ansible plugins. Throughout this chapter, we discussed various types of plugins in detail, both from the implementation point and on a code level. The chapter also demonstrated how to write sample plugins by writing custom lookup and callback plugins. You should now be able to write your own custom plugins for Ansible.

The next chapter will explore how to configure Ansible and fit together everything that has been discussed up until now. The chapter will also guide you on how to share your plugins and roles and explore some best practices to follow.

6

Fitting It All Together – Integration

By the time you reach this chapter, you will have successfully created your own custom modules and plugins as per your requirements. Now, you might find yourself wondering, what next?

Ansible is a great community product. It provides a number of modules and plugins for everyone to use. Now that you are familiar with the Python API, have already written an Ansible module and probably a plugin, too, it's time to give back to the community. Since you had some requirements that could not be met by the native Ansible, chances are that other people are also in need of further help. Let's look at various ways in which one can give back to the community.

This chapter will cover how to configure Ansible to integrate your modules in the existing Ansible library. The chapter will also cover how you can distribute your modules and help improve Ansible.

Configuring Ansible

To take full advantage of Ansible, it is necessary to configure Ansible properly. Although stock settings are sufficient for most users, power users may want to tweak things and make a few changes.

Global persistent settings are defined in the Ansible configuration file located at `/etc/ansible/ansible.cfg`. However, you can also place custom configuration files in the root of the Ansible play or in the home directory of the user. Settings can also be changed by setting environment variables.

With so many ways to configure Ansible, an important question arises – how does Ansible prioritize the configuration file? How does it choose which configuration to use during a playbook execution?

In Ansible version 1.9, configurations are processed in the following order:

- `ANSIBLE_CONFIG`: Environment variable
- `ansible.cfg`: Current working directory from where Ansible is called
- `.ansible.cfg`: Configuration file stored in the user's home directory
- `/etc/ansible/ansible.cfg`: Default configuration file in case no other configuration is found

Ansible will process the configurations in the above order. Whichever configuration is found first will be used during execution. To keep everything clean, Ansible does not merge the configuration files. All the files are kept separate.

Environment configuration

By setting environment variables, you can override any existing configurations loaded from the configuration file. In the present version of Ansible, environment configurations take the top most priority. To find the complete list of environment variables supported by Ansible, you need to look into the source code. The following list contains a few environment variables you should know in order to get your modules and plugins working:

Environment variable	Default value
ANSIBLE_ACTION_PLUGINS	~/.ansible/plugins/action:/usr/share/ansible/plugins/action
ANSIBLE_CACHE_PLUGINS	~/.ansible/plugins/cache:/usr/share/ansible/plugins/cache
ANSIBLE_CALLBACK_PLUGINS	~/.ansible/plugins/callback:/usr/share/ansible/plugins/callback
ANSIBLE_CONNECTION_PLUGINS	~/.ansible/plugins/connection:/usr/share/ansible/plugins/connection
ANSIBLE_LOOKUP_PLUGINS	~/.ansible/plugins/lookup:/usr/share/ansible/plugins/lookup
ANSIBLE_INVENTORY_PLUGINS	~/.ansible/plugins/inventory:/usr/share/ansible/plugins/inventory
ANSIBLE_VARS_PLUGINS	~/.ansible/plugins/vars:/usr/share/ansible/plugins/vars

Environment variable	Default value
ANSIBLE_FILTER_PLUGINS	~/.ansible/plugins/filter:/usr/share/ansible/plugins/filter
ANSIBLE_KEEP_REMOTE_FILES	False
ANSIBLE_PRIVATE_KEY_FILE	None

Fun fact

If you have cowsay installed on the management node, Ansible playbook runs will use cowsay and make the output more interesting. If you don't want cowsay enabled, simply set nocows=0 in the configuration file.

Contributing to Ansible

Before starting to contribute to Ansible, it is important to know where and how to contribute and what to contribute. To reduce duplication of effort, you need to stay in touch with the community. There might be instances in which a feature you want to work on is already being worked on by someone else, or perhaps a bug you think you can fix is picked up by someone else and is currently being worked upon. Also, there may arise situations when you need some help from the community in finishing off some task; maybe you are stuck at some point and have a few unanswered questions. This is where community comes into play. Ansible has its own IRC channel and mailing list for such purposes.

You can join the *#ansible* channel on irc.freenode.net, where you can talk to the community members, discuss features, and get help. This is where people live chat with each other. However, since Ansible is a global community, not all members will be available around the clock, and it might so happen your question remains unanswered. If so, you can drop an e-mail to the mailing list where the question is more likely to get the attention of core developers and advanced users.

You may want to join the following mailing lists:

- **The Ansible Project list**: https://groups.google.com/forum/#!forum/ansible-project (a general user discussion mailing list for sharing Ansible tips and asking questions)

- **The Ansible Development list**: https://groups.google.com/forum/#!forum/ansible-devel (discuss features in progress, suggest feature requests, get help extending Ansible)

- **The Ansible Anounce list**: https://groups.google.com/forum/#!forum/ansible-announce (A read-only list that shares information about the new releases of Ansible)

Ansible is an open source project hosted on GitHub. Anyone having a GitHub account can contribute to the Ansible project. The project takes in contributions through GitHub pull requests.

Galaxy–sharing roles

Writing a playbook for a task you want to automate helps you save time and effort every time you have to deploy. This can also save time for others if you can share the roles with the community.

Ansible provides a great platform to share your plays. Galaxy is a platform where you can share your pre-packaged units of work as "roles," which can be integrated or dropped into the playbooks and used. Some roles can be dropped in directly, while others may require a bit of tweaking. What's more, that Galaxy provides a reliability score against each shared role. You can choose from a number of available roles, rate them, and comment on them.

Roles are hosted on GitHub. Galaxy allows integration with GitHub, and you can use your existing GitHub account to log into Galaxy and share the roles. To share your role, create a GitHub repository, clone it, and initialize a Galaxy role in the cloned repository. This can be done with the following bit of code:

```
$ ansible-galaxy init <role-name> --force
```

This will create a directory structure needed to organize the code. You can then use this directory structure to create an Ansible role. Once you have your role ready, test it in a playbook, and verify if it's working as expected. You might then push it to the GitHub repository.

To upload the code to Galaxy, you need to log in to the Galaxy platform (https://galaxy.ansible.com) using your GitHub account. By using the **Add a Role** option from the menu and supplying the required credentials, Galaxy will import the role from your GitHub repository and make it available on the Galaxy platform for the entire community.

You might also want to apply tags to your repository, which Galaxy, by default, treats as version numbers. This allows users to choose between different versions. If there are no tags specified, users will always be able to download only the latest available code on your GitHub repository.

Galaxy – best practices

While writing any role you may want to share through Galaxy, there are a few best practices that should be followed in order to ensure everything runs smoothly for the end user:

- Always document whatever you make and place it in the `README.md` file. This is the file the end user refers to while using the role.

- Include and list all the dependencies explicitly. Never assume anything.

- Prefix the variables with the role name.

- Test the role before you share it. The more testing you perform, the less chances of it being broken.

These best practices also apply to any contribution you make in general to Ansible. Whether you are developing a module or plugin, or are writing a role that you plan to share with the community, these practices ensure everything runs smoothly. Though it's not mandatory, it is highly recommended to follow these best practices in order to make the contribution easy for others, as well as to understand and extend later whenever required.

Sharing modules and plugins

By this stage, you will have developed your own Ansible module or plugin. Now, you want to share it with both your friends and strangers and help them simplify their tasks. You might also want to collaborate on developing a module or plugin and require help from the general public.

One of the great developer collaboration platforms is GitHub. You can create a repository on GitHub and push your code to it. You might accompany your module code with an Ansible playbook, demonstrating how to use the module or plugin you just developed.

GitHub allows people to contribute to one single project. It's usually a good idea to put your code online on GitHub, for it provides a number of advantages. Other than encouraging a collaborative nature, it provides version control, where you can roll back your changes if required, as well as track any changes made to the code base in the past. While collaborating, you might choose which pull request to address and which to ignore by going through the proposed change, thus allowing you control over your repository.

Getting a module into Ansible

Ansible modules are hosted in two separate subrepositories of Ansible, namely:

- `ansible-modules-core`
- `ansible-modules-extras`

The module repository, `ansible-modules-core`, contains the most popular modules that are shipped with Ansible. These are the core modules that are used most and are essential to address basic functionalities of a system. The repository contains almost every essential feature required for Ansible to function properly. This repository does not take in module submissions directly. However, you can report and fix bugs if you come across any.

The module repository, `ansible-modules-extras`, is a subset of `ansible-modules` that contains modules of a lower priority (that is, modules that cannot be considered core modules). New modules are submitted to this repository. Depending on the popularity and completeness of the module, a module can be promoted to the core modules.

Ansible, being an open source project hosted on GitHub, takes in contributions by means of GitHub pull requests. To get your modules into Ansible you need to understand how the GitHub pull request works:

- Fork the Ansible project from `https://github.com/ansible/ansible-modules-extras` or `https://github.com/ansible/ansible-modules-core` to your GitHub account.

- File an issue on `https://github.com/ansible/ansible-modules-extras/issues` or `https://github.com/ansible/ansible-modules-core/issues` for the feature you are tying to address. If you are trying to fix a bug, an issue should already exist against the bug. If not, create one and assign it to yourself.

- Push in your module or the patch to fix a bug against the bug number you just created.

- Raise a pull request to the source repository (that is, Ansible).

Once done, the reviewers will verify the code, review it, and check if it addresses the issue. You might receive some reviews or change requests after the review that you'll have to fix. There might be multiple iterations before your code gets merged.

If your module or plugin is merged in the Ansible repository, it will be available to all Ansible users with the next release.

Getting plugins into Ansible

As discussed in the previous chapter, Ansible plugins are categorized as per their function into different groups such as action, callback, lookup, and so on. Unlike modules, Ansible plugins are a part of the Ansible repository itself. There are no different repositories like extras and core. You can directly open an issue in the Ansible repository, discuss it over the mailing list, and put up a pull request upon approval.

The following link lists the existing plugins in the Ansible repository:

```
https://github.com/ansible/ansible/tree/devel/lib/ansible/plugins
```

Points to remember

When submitting a new module, there are a few things one should keep in mind:

- Always discuss the feature you are proposing. This will help you save time and effort in case the feature is already being worked upon.
- Not all features you propose will be accepted. There will always be a call on the use case and what the module/plugin brings.
- It's good practice to maintain the module/plugin you have written.
- Be active in picking up and fixing any bugs that are reported against your module. This will make your module more reliable.
- Make your module as generic as possible (that is, it should accept user arguments and adapt accordingly, providing the user with more flexibility). Although, it should focus on one particular task for which it was created. This increases the chances of acceptance.

Best practices

By now, you should be both familiar and comfortable working with the Ansible Python API. You may even have your own Ansible modules or plugins that you want to share with the community. The following are a few best practices you should follow when sharing your modules, plugins, and roles with the community:

- Always test your module before submitting a pull request.
- Make your modules as generic as possible.
- Always document whatever you create, be it a module, plugin, or an Ansible role that you share across Galaxy.
- List down any dependencies explicitly.
- Keep the discussion going on the mailing list and IRC channels. Being an active member gets you more visibility.

Summary

This chapter covered topics like configuring your Ansible environment and how to get your modules and plugins into the Ansible repository. It also touched upon how you can distribute your module through Git. This chapter also introduced you to the Galaxy platform, a service provided by Ansible to share your roles. The chapter also gave pointers on best practices and various things you should keep in mind while submitting your module.

The next chapter will take you through a series of scenarios where Ansible can come in handy. The chapter will also integrate everything that has been covered thus far in the previous chapters, combine it all, and present a scenario that will give you an idea of how you can use Ansible to its full effect.

7
Becoming a Master – A Complete Configuration Guide

By the time you reach this chapter, you will have had already gone through all the concepts that are in the scope of this book. This chapter will build upon everything learned from the previous chapters, use some basics, and present you with real-life use cases where Ansible can come in handy. The chapter will show you how you can use Ansible to solve simple, as well as complex, problems and scenarios.

One playbook, different applications, multiple targets

You might come across scenarios where different environments need different settings or deployment steps, for example, deploying to different environments such as Development, QA, Stage, or Production. There might be small changes in the deployment scheme, for instance, a QA instance of a web application points to a local instance of a database, while the Production deployment points to a different database server.

Another scenario could be one in which you are to deploy an application that you built for different distributions (for example, those that are RPM based and Debian based). In this scenario, deployment will be different, as both the platforms use different application managers. RPM based distributions use the Yum or DNF package management utility, while Debian based distributions use the DPKG utility for package management. Also, the resultant package that is created will be different – one is .rpm while the other is .deb.

In this scenario, even through the target platform is different and the deployment schemes or configurations differ from each other, all these can be handled in one playbook by means of defining roles.

Let's move to a few practical scenarios. In the first scenario, you need to deploy an application consisting of a backend database (MySQL) and a frontend web application. The web application queries the backend database and serves the data as requested by the user. Both the web application and MySQL database are to be deployed on different machines.

Let's divide the installation and configuration tasks into two categories:

- **System preparation**: This is a common task for both the web application system and database server. Both systems need to first be prepared for installation. Preparation might involve tasks like configuring repositories and updating the system.
- **Deploy**: This includes deploying both the database and web application, followed by any configuration changes that are required.

If you analyze the categories, system preparation is common to both the systems, while the deploy jobs are specific to each application. In such a scenario, you can segregate the jobs into roles. You can have three roles – one "common" role, which executes on both the machines, and one role each for both the database and web application, respectively. This makes the Ansible playbook more modular and easy to maintain.

The following is an Ansible playbook based on the above analysis of the problem statement:

db-webapp-role.yaml

```
---

- hosts: all
  user: root
  roles:
    - { role: common }

- hosts: database
  user: root
  roles:
    - { role: database }

- hosts: webapp
  user: root
  roles:
    - { role: webapp }
```

The preceding playbook calls different roles – common, webapp, and database and executes them on the corresponding host groups. The common role is executed on all the host groups (that is, on both webapp and database). This is then followed by executing the individual roles on specific host groups. The following are the roles that are called by the preceding play:

Role : common

```
---
- name: Create hosts file for each machine
  template: src hosts.j2 dest=/etc/hosts

- name: Copy Repo file
  copy: src=local-tree.repo dest=/etc/yum.repos.d/

- name: Update the system
  yum: name=* state=latest
```

This is a common role, which will be executed on all the target hosts. It configures a repository that serves packages and dependencies to the target machine. The role configures this repository and updates all the packages installed on the target machine to their latest versions.

The following role will be executed only on the hosts specified under the database group in the inventory file. This will install the MySQL database and copy over a configuration file, which will configure the database and create the required tables on the target host. It will also ensure the MYSQL service is running on the target host. As per the Ansible play, this role will be executed on the target host post successful completion of the common role:

Role: database

```
---
- name: Install MySQL databse server
  yum: name=mysql state=present

- name: Start MySQL service
  service: name=mysqld status=started

- name: Create a directory to copy the setup script
  file: path=/temp/configdb state=directory mode=0755

- name: Copy script to create database tables
  copy: src=configdb.sh dest=/temp/configdb

- name: Run configdb.sh to create database tables
  shell: configdb.sh chdir=/temp/configdb
```

The following role is specific to deploying the web application on the webapp group of hosts in the inventory file. The role will execute upon successful completion of the common role as per the Ansible play:

Role: webapp

```
---
- name: Install HTTP server
  yum: name=httpd state=present

- name: Start httpd service
  service: name=httpd state=started

- name: Create temporary directory to copy over the rpm
  file: path=/temp/webapp state=directory mode=0755

- name: Copy the application package to the target machine
  copy: src=webapp-2.4.16-1.fc22.x86_64 dest=/temp/webapp

- name: Install the webapp
  command: yum install -y ./webapp-2.4.16-1.fc22.x86_64 chdir=/temp/
webapp

- name: Copy configuration script
  copy: src=configweb.sh dest=/temp/webapp

- name: Execute the configuration script
  shell: configweb.sh chdir=/temp/webapp
```

Ansible roles – using tags

Ansible playbooks are meant to be modular and capable of being used in different environments whenever required. For this purpose, roles were introduced. However, just using roles may not be enough, as you may want to use different roles for different environments on the same host. Okay, this sounds confusing. Let's dive into a scenario.

You can integrate your Ansible playbooks with your continuous deployment system, which helps developers deploy the application whenever they want during the development cycle. During this cycle, they might want to set up the system and configure the application in a manner appropriate to the stage of development. Since the application is being developed, not all features may be complete while deploying on the development environment. However, once the application is complete, the developer might want to do a complete run of Ansible to replicate the production or QE environment, thus ensuring the application runs with all the settings as required on the production host. In this case, there are two different environments–development and QE-ready.

Since the deployment is done on the same host, and there are multiple roles that can be executed, you can use tags. You can couple a role with a tag. Thus, by specifying the tag from the command line, Ansible knows which role to execute.

One simple way to demonstrate this is as follows. Let's say you have an application which, when required to be deployed in a development environment, you clone the code from your Git Hub repository and run the `install.sh` script. Also in the development environment, you have some relaxed security policies, say SeLinux is set to permissive mode. The same application, when passed to QE, should be packaged in RPM and then installed. Also, the security relaxations are not allowed, hence SeLinux needs to stay in enforcing mode. Since a developer will have one development instance, he or she will have to execute both the roles on the same instance. In this case, the developer can use tags to use different roles as and when required for deploying the application.

The following is an Ansible playbook along with the roles that demonstrate the preceding scenario:

Role : `development`

```
---

- name: Create directory to clone git repo
  file: path=/tmp/gitrepo state=directory mode=0755

- name: Clone Git repo
  git: repo={{ item }} dest=/tmp/gitrepo
  with_items:
    - "{{ git_repo }}"

- name: Set selinux to permissive
  selinux: policy=targeted state=permissive

- name: Run install.sh to deploy application
  shell: install.sh chdir=/tmp/gitrepo/example
```

Role : `qe_ready`

```
---

- name: Make directory to store RPM
  file: path=/tmp/deploy state=directory mode=0755

- name: Download the RPM to Directory
  get_url: url={{ item }} dest=/tmp/deploy
  with_items:
```

```
      - "{{ rpm_link }}"

  - name: Install RPM
    command: yum install -y *.rpm chdir=/tmp/deploy

  - name: Set Selinux to Enforcing
    selinux: policy=targeted state=enforcing
```

The preceding two roles are a part of the same Ansible playbook and will be called as per required based on the tag you specify. The following Ansible play demonstrates how to bind a role to a specific tag:

Ansible Play : `demo-tag.yaml`

```
    ---

  - hosts: application
    user: rdas
    sudo: yes
    roles:
      - { role: development, tags: ['development'] }
      - { role: qe_ready, tags: ['qe'] }
```

The `development` role is now binded to the `development` tag while the `qe_ready` role is binded to the `qe` tag. An Ansible playbook can be executed by specifying tags using the `-t` flag in the following manner:

```
# ansible-playbook -i hosts -t development demo-tag.yaml
```

Getting infrastructure information and hosting it centrally

In the previous chapters, you created a `dmidecode` module that collected system information from the target machines and returned a JSON output. The module also allowed you to toggle a flag "save" to `true` if you wished to store the output in a JSON file on the target machine itself.

Storing system information on respective target machines does not serve much purpose, as the data still resides on the target machines, and to access the data, one needs to log in to a different machine and then parse the respective JSON files. To handle this, the book introduced you to callbacks, which help get back the JSON data and store it as JSON files on the controller node (that is, the node from where you are executing the Ansible playbook).

However, even after doing so, the problem is not completely resolved. You did manage to collect the data from your infrastructure nodes, but accessibility still remains an issue.

- One needs access to the controller machine to access all the files

- In a real-world scenario, you cannot grant access to everyone

- Even if you plan to give access to select individuals, your availability remains a bottleneck

To handle this, one solution can be to host all these JSON files to a central server from where one can download the required JSON files, parse them, and generate reports. A better solution to this problem, however, can be to index the data in a central Elasticsearch instance, which then serves the data over a RESTful API.

 Elasticsearch is an open source search engine built on top of Apache Lucene. Elasticsearch is written in Java and uses Lucene internally for indexing and searching. It aims to make full-text search easy by hiding the complexities of Lucene behind a simple RESTful API.

Source: Elasticsearch documentation from `www.elastic.co`.

This chapter will not go into depth about what Elasticsearch is and how it functions, as this is beyond the scope of this book. For details about Elasticsearch, you can refer to either the online documentation or *Mastering ElasticSearch* (`https://www.packtpub.com/web-development/mastering-elasticsearch-second-edition`), published by *Packt Publishing*.

Back to the issue of indexing data in Elasticsearch and serving it over an HTTP, API can be a solution to the problem at hand. For this to work, you'll have to write a callback plugin that interacts with an Elasticsearch instance and indexes the JSON data, which can then be served over API. Python provides a library, `pyes`, to interact with an Elasticsearch instance.

Let's name the callback plugin `loges.py` and store it in the `callback_plugins` directory in the root of the Ansible play, as shown in the following code:

```
from pyes import *
import json

# Change this to your Elasticsearch URL
ES_URL = '10.3.10.183:9200'

def index_elasticsearch(host, result):
    ''' index results in elasticsearch '''
```

```
    # Create connection object to Elasticsearch instance
    conn = ES(ES_URL)
    # Create index 'infra' if not present. Used for the first function
call
    if not conn.indices.exists_index('infra'):
        conn.indices.create_index('infra')
    # Index results in Elasticsearch.
    # infra: index name
    # dmidecode: document type
    # host: ID
    conn.index(result, 'infra', 'dmidecode', host)
    print 'Data added to Elasticsearch'

class CallbackModule(object):
    '''
    This adds the result JSON to ElasticSearch database
    '''
    def runner_on_ok(self, host, result):
        try:
            if result['var']['dmi_data[\'msg\']']:
                index_elasticsearch(host, result['var']['dmi_
data[\'msg\']'])
        except:
            pass
```

Post creating this callback plugin, if you run the Ansible play `dmidecode.yaml`, upon successful run, the JSON output will be indexed in the Elasticsearch instance and should be available through the API. Data will be indexed in the index named `infra` with the document type `dmidecode`. Every indexed document will have a unique ID, which, in this case, would be the `Hostname` or `IP`, whichever is applicable.

Creating a dynamic inventory of just launched instances

An Ansible playbook, or even individual modules, are executed against target hosts commonly specified in an inventory file. Their most basic use is to have a static inventory file (for example, hosts) containing a list of all the target host IPs or hostnames against which the Ansible play has to be executed. However, in the real world, things might not be this dead simple. For instance, you might be required to launch a new instance on Cloud – say OpenStack or AWS – or launch a basic virtual machine and then deploy your application using the Ansible playbook. In this case, the target IP is unknown until the instance is launched, and therefore a static inventory file would not serve the purpose.

One of the major benefits of running Ansible programmatically and using the Ansible API was to handle runtime variables such as the target IP, in this case. This is a scenario where you can take full advantage of using the Python API to run the Ansible playbook while creating a dynamic inventory.

For generating a dynamic inventory file, the Jinja2 template can be used. Jinja2 is fully supported by Ansible and can be used to create any template you want. Jinja2 is a vast topic in itself and cannot be covered in detail, as it is beyond the scope of this book. However, this specific scenario will touch upon Jinja2 and how it can be used in conjunction with Ansible. In the above case, the Jinja2 template will be used to render the inventory file at runtime.

Let's revisit the example from *Chapter 4*, *Exploring API*, where an Ansible playbook, webserver.yaml, was programmatically executed on an inventory file, hosts. Contrary to the example in *Chapter 4*, *Exploring API*, the inventory file will be rendered at runtime in the following example. This comes in handy while performing end-to-end automation, starting from launching instances and deploying applications.

```python
from ansible.playbook import PlayBook
from ansible.inventory import Inventory
from ansible import callbacks
from ansible import utils

import jinja2
from tempfile import NamedTemporaryFile
import os

# Boilerplace callbacks for stdout/stderr and log output

utils.VERBOSITY = 0
playbook_cb = callbacks.PlaybookCallbacks(verbose=utils.VERBOSITY)
stats = callbacks.AggregateStats()
runner_cb = callbacks.PlaybookRunnerCallbacks(stats, verbose=utils.
VERBOSITY)

# [Mock] Launch instance and return instance IP

def launch_instance(number):
    '''
    Launch instances on OpenStack and return a list of instance IPs

    args:
        number: Number of instances to launch
    return:
```

```
        target: List containing IPs of launched instances

    This is a dummy function and does not contain code for launching
instances
    Launching an instance on OpenStack, AWS or a virtual machine is
beyond the
    scope of this book. The example focuses on creating a dynamic
inventory
    file to be used by Ansible.
    '''
    # return 2 IPs as the caller requested launching 2 instances.
    target = ['192.168.10.20', '192.168.10.25']
    return target


# Dynamic Inventory

inventory = """
[remote]
{% for elem in public_ip_address  %}
{{ elem }}
{% endfor %}
"""
target = launch_instance(2)
inventory_template = jinja2.Template(inventory)
rendered_inventory = inventory_template.render({
    'public_ip_address' : target
})

# Create a temporary file and write the template string to it
hosts = NamedTemporaryFile(delete=False)
hosts.write(rendered_inventory)
hosts.close()

pb = PlayBook(
    playbook = 'webserver.yaml',
    host_list = hosts.name,
    remote_user = 'rdas',
    stats = stats,
    callbacks=playbook_cb,
    runner_callbacks=runner_cb,
    private_key_file='id_rsa.pem'
)
```

```
results = pb.run()

playbook_cb.on_stats(pb.stats)

print results
```

In the preceding example, the `launch_instance` function is only used to represent some code that can launch an instance or a virtual machine. The function, when called, returns a list of IPs associated with the launched instances. The returned list is cached in a variable, `target`, and is then used to render the inventory file. The following code section...:

```
inventory = """
[remote]
{% for elem in public_ip_address  %}
{{ elem }}
{% endfor %}
"""
```

...is the Jinja2 template that is rendered by using the following code:

```
inventory_template = jinja2.Template(inventory)
rendered_inventory = inventory_template.render({
    'public_ip_address' : target
})
```

The rendered inventory is then written into a temporary file using the following piece of code:

```
hosts = NamedTemporaryFile(delete=False)
hosts.write(rendered_inventory)
hosts.close()
```

This creates an inventory file at runtime with IPs of the target machines (newly launched instances), as returned by the `launch_instance` method.

Ansible through a bastion host

In the real world, production servers are normally configured to prevent SSH connections from outside their own private network. This is to reduce the number of possible attack vectors and also to keep the access point to a bare minimum. This helps in limiting access, creating better logging, and increases security. This is a common security practice and is implemented by using a bastion host.

A bastion host is specifically designed to withstand attacks. Normally, the bastion host runs only one service. Other services are either removed or disabled in order to minimize threats.

In this scenario, with a bastion host coming into the picture, Ansible is not able to directly SSH to the target host from the controller node. It needs to proxy its commands through the bastion host in order to reach the target machine.

To achieve this, all you need is to modify three files in your Ansible play root directory:

- `hosts`: Inventory file
- `ansible.cfg`: Ansible's configuration files
- `ssh.cfg`: SSH configurations

The inventory file includes a group, `bastion`, alongside the usual target hosts. The following code is a sample inventory `hosts` file:

```
[bastion]
10.68.214.8

[database_servers]
172.16.10.5
172.16.10.6
```

Since Ansible uses SSH for almost all its operations, the next step is to configure SSH. SSH by itself allows us to customize the settings as per the requirement. To configure SSH for this particular Ansible play, you need to create an `ssh.cfg` file with the following contents in the root of the Ansible playbook:

```
Host 172.16.*
    ProxyCommand  ssh -q -A rdas@10.68.214.8 nc %h:%p
Host *
    ControlMaster    auto
    ControlPath     ~/.ssh/mux-%r@%h:%p
    ControlPersist    15m
```

The preceding SSH configuration proxies all the commands to the nodes in network `172.16.*` through our Bastion host `10.68.214.8`. The control setting `ControlPersist` allows SSH to reuse the already established connection, thus improving performance and speeding up the Ansible playbook execution.

Now that the SSH is configured, you need to tell Ansible to use this SSH configuration. For this, you need to create an `ansible.cfg` file in the root of the Ansible play with the following contents:

```
[ssh_connection]
ssh_args = -F ssh.cfg
control_path = ~/.ssh/mux-%r@%h:%p
```

Ansible will now use the above configuration to use `ssh.cfg` as the SSH configuration file and hence proxy the commands through the bastion host.

Happy managers = happy you

Up until this point, this chapter has been about implementing Ansible for management, deployment, and configuration. Well, there is one more point that still remains – reporting.

At the end of a long playbook execution, you may have the application deployed and you may have the audit data for your infrastructure or anything that the playbook was designed to do. Additionally, you can have logs for the playbook execution. However, let's say that at the end of day, you are asked to provide a report. You now have to sit down and create reports and fill out an Excel spreadsheet, as this is what your manager demands – an overview of the state of things as they are. This is something that can again be achieved by extending Ansible.

So, you did a playbook run and what you get is run logs on `stdout`. The question now becomes: how do you make an Excel report out of it? Yes, you guessed it right – the callback plugin comes to the rescue. You can write your own custom callback plugins that can help you record your Ansible play results and create a spreadsheet out of them. This would reduce the overhead task of creating reports manually.

The report might vary for different use cases, as not one single report fits all. Hence, you will have to write callback plugins for the different kinds of report you want to generate. Some prefer an HTML-based report, while some prefer Excel spreadsheets.

The following example reuses the `dmidecode` module from *Chapter 3*, *Digging Deeper into Ansible Modules*. The module is used to generate a JSON output, which is good for machine processing. However, JSON is not something one would like to read through manually for a report. Representing the data in an Excel spreadsheet makes much more sense, while creating a report as a spreadsheet is more reader-friendly and gives the complete picture at a glance. Someone with a non-technical background can also read data from an Excel sheet without much hassle.

The following is a callback module that creates an Excel sheet, reads the JSON output generated by executing the `dmidecode` module, and appends data for each host in the Excel spreadsheet. It is written in Python and uses the `openpyxl` library to create the Excel spreadsheet.

```
#!/bin/python
import openpyxl
import json
```

```
import os

PATH = '/tmp'

def create_report_file():
    ''' Create the initial workbook if not exists
    '''
    os.chdir(PATH)
    wb = openpyxl.Workbook()
    sheet = wb.get_active_sheet()
    sheet.title = 'Infrastructure'
    sheet['A1'] = 'Machine IP'
    sheet['B1'] = 'Serial No'
    sheet['C1'] = 'Manufacturer'
    fname = 'Infra-Info.xlsx'
    wb.save(fname)
    return fname

def write_data(host, serial_no, manufacturer):
    ''' Write data to Excel '''
    os.chdir(PATH)
    wb = openpyxl.load_workbook('Infra-Info.xlsx')
    sheet = wb.get_sheet_by_name('Infrastructure')
    rowNum = sheet.max_row + 1
    sheet.cell(row=rowNum, column=1).value = host
    sheet.cell(row=rowNum, column=2).value = serial_no
    sheet.cell(row=rowNum, column=3).value = manufacturer
    wb.save('tmp-Infra-Info.xlsx')

def rename_file():
    os.chdir(PATH)
    os.remove('Infra-Info.xlsx')
    os.rename('tmp-Infra-Info.xlsx', 'Infra-Info.xlsx')


def extract_data(host, result_json):
    ''' Write data to the sheet
    '''
    serial_no = result_json['Hardware Specs']['System']['Serial
Number']
```

```
        manufacturer = result_json['Hardware Specs']['System']
['Manufacturer']
        if not os.path.exists('/tmp/Infra-Info.xlsx'):
            create_report_file()
        write_data(host, serial_no, manufacturer)
        rename_file()



class CallbackModule(object):

    def runner_on_ok(self, host, result):
        try:
            if result['var']['dmi_data[\'msg\']']:
                extract_data(host, result['var']['dmi_data[\'msg\']'])
        except:
            pass
```

The preceding callback module is just an example of how you can represent data in an Excel spreadsheet and generate reports. The callback module can be extended to fill in more details as required in the report. The preceding module only adds the host, serial number, and manufacturer of the host machine.

Please note that since the above callback module appends data to the same Excel spreadsheet, Ansible should execute tasks one host at a time. Therefore, you should set the fork as 1.

This can be done by using the --forks flag. The following bit of code is how the Ansible playbook was executed:

```
ansible-playbook -i hosts dmidecode.yaml --forks 1
```

Here is the generated Excel report:

A	B	C
Machine IP	Serial No	Manufacturer
192.168.1.15	SGH306S5BC	Hewlett-Packard
192.168.1.18	SGH324PMHX	Hewlett-Packard
192.168.1.19	SGH316S5BD	Hewlett-Packard
192.168.1.23	PC07VS1W	LENOVO

Summary

This chapter took you through various real-life scenarios in which Ansible can be used and how you can extend Ansible to suit your needs. The chapter started with the basics of Ansible such as defining roles and using tags. The chapter then gradually progressed to more complex scenarios, building upon examples from the previous chapters. The chapter also included a very common scenario in which Ansible required custom configurations in order to proxy the tasks through a bastion host. The chapter also gave you an idea of how you can exploit Ansible to automate some routine tasks like reporting.

Overall, this chapter combined everything learned from the previous chapters and provided real-life scenarios and use cases of the same.

Index

A

Ansible
  about 59
  configuring 59, 60
  contributing to 5, 61
  diving into 4
  environment configuration 60
  exploiting 29
  extending 8
  extending, reasons 3, 4
  features 2
  modules, obtaining into 64
  plugins, obtaining into 65
Ansible Anounce list
  reference link 62
Ansible architecture 5
Ansible code
  reference link 5
Ansible components
  callback 5, 8
  connection 5, 6
  facts 7
  inventory 5
  modules 5
  playbook 7
  runner 5-7
  variables 7
Ansible Development list
  reference link 61
Ansible module
  writing 11
AnsibleModule boilerplate 20-33
Ansible modules
  about 11
  creating, in Python 20

Ansible Project list
  reference link 61
arguments
  reading 15-17

B

basic Bash module
  writing 12-14
bastion host 77, 78
best practices, modules 25

C

callback plugins
  about 52, 53
  reference link 52
callbacks 5, 8, 38, 42
callbacks operations
  AggregateStats 43
  CliRunnerCallbacks 43
  DefaultRunnerCallbacks 43
  PlaybookCallbacks 43
  PlaybookRunnerCallbacks 43
complex arguments
  about 34
  reading 34, 35
conditions
  filters, using with 56
configurations, Ansible
  CWD 29
  ENV 29
  global configuration file 29
  HOME 29
connection 5

Printed in Poland
by Amazon Fulfillment
Poland Sp. z o.o., Wrocław